THE PARADISE
MAN

THE PARADISE
MAN

ACCORDING TO THOMAS MERTON

LINHXUAN VU

Library of Congress Control Number: 2016916661
ISBN: Hardcover   978-1-5245-4973-2
             Softcover   978-1-5245-4972-5
             eBook   978-1-5245-4971-8

Print information available on the last page.

Rev. date: 10/12/2016

To order additional copies of this book, contact:
Xlibris
1-888-795-4274
www.Xlibris.com
Orders@Xlibris.com
735857

CONTENTS

ACKNOWLEDGEMENTS

Grateful acknowledgement is made to
my professors of Dominican Province in
Vietnam, of Western Dominican Province in
California and of Graduate Theological Union
in Berkeley, California; to professors and
friends who gave advice on my manuscript:
Fr. Cyprian Harrison, Fr. Paul Jones,
Fr. David Garrick, Fr. Neil Arce,
Prof. Wayne Lobue,
Writer Dave Malone,
Writer David Keys, Mike Cronin,
Atty. John Paul Douglas,
Prof. John Ockels, Ms. Rose Brower.
Grateful acknowledgement is made
to all publishers, authors,
copy right owners of the works quoted in this book.
Special gratitude is made to sponsors of this book:
Mr. & Mrs. Nguyen Ngoc Ky, MD

**To Peter Vu Dinh Hao
and
Maria Pham Thi Hong Vy
Parents who gave me
the happiest days
of life**

*"Paradise is all around us
and we do not understand. It is
wide open. The sword is
taken away, but we do not know
it; we are off "one to
his farm and another to his merchandise"* [1]

Thomas Merton

INTRODUCTION

INTRODUCTION

Since Adam and Eve left Eden, humanity has endured through long millennia of hardships and sufferings, especially death. But the hearts of their children and great grandchildren have never given up the hope that someday they could return to the place of happiness which once had been their inheritance. It is a legitimate and dignified dream. In fact, since the day Adam and Eve left, paradise has remained on earth waiting for every single human child to return.

Following the great journey of humankind in the search for the paradise, utopias and fairytale worlds expressed in many centuries in various cultures and religions, this present work describes the arrival of the search that means paradise is found. We seek to understand what is the life of the Paradise Man? What is the Paradise World?

Pope Francis of the Roman Catholic Church spoke to the US Congress on September 24, 2015, and he gave praise to four great Americans: Abraham Lincoln, Martin Luther King Jr., Dorothy Day and Thomas Merton. The last of these four great heroes, Thomas Merton, will be the lead contributor for this work.

Thomas Merton (1915-1968) is recognized as the most influential American Catholic author of the twentieth century. His autobiography, *The Seven Storey Mountain,* has sold over one million copies and has been translated into over fifteen languages. He wrote over sixty books and many poems and articles on various topics. The most central themes are the monastic life and contemplative prayer. He was also a strong supporter of the nonviolent civil rights movement. Thomas Merton was born on January 31st, 1915 in Prades, France, to a New Zealand father and an American mother. Both were artists. Merton converted to Roman Catholicism whilst at Columbia University in 1942. He was called to priesthood and entered the Abbey of Gethsemani in Kentucky, a community of Trappist monks, the most ascetic Roman Catholic monastic order. In Gethsemani Abbey he lived for twenty-seven years and went through profound ongoing conversion.

During his last years, he became deeply interested in Asian religions. The Dalai Lama praised him as having more profound understanding of Buddhism than any other Christian he had known. He died in Bangkok on December 10th, 1968 by an accidental electrocution during a conference on East-West monastic dialogue. [2]

Thomas Merton left in many of his writings profound observations concerning the noble human dream and in particular he introduced us to the paradise of the Desert Fathers:

> **Modern studies of the Fathers have revealed beyond question that one of the main motives that impelled men to embrace the "angelic life" (bios angelikos) of solitude and poverty in the desert was precisely the hope that by so doing they might return to paradise. [3]**

Thomas Merton wrote the above lines in his book: *Zen and the Birds of Appetite*. This book was Merton's dialogue with Dr. Daisetz Suzuki, the famous Japanese scholar and writer, about the transcendent experience of paradise in both Christian and Buddhist traditions. Thomas Merton openheartedly shared more with us what he found: **"Paradise is not 'heaven.' Paradise is a state, or indeed a place, on earth. Paradise belongs more properly to the present than to the future life."4**

Paradise! What is it like? It is not a material paradise providing bodily satisfaction and mental relaxation like that of vacation locations: Hawaii, Miami, Las Vegas and Hollywood. It also is not the paradise of Milton, which has been said by E.M.W. Tillyard to be too weak and unconvincing because it has "too much leisure and . . . nothing to do." He also compared Adam and Eve in Milton's work to "old age pensioners enjoying a perpetual youth."5 The paradise which Merton talked about was the paradise of the Desert Fathers.

Merton's paradise, in the last analysis, is on earth, but it is an interior place. It is rather an attitude of heart, a state of consciousness, in a spiritual journey. The recovery of paradise occurs when the ego in us becomes empty like a desert. The more the noisy ego diminishes, the more the paradise appears in all its beauty. In fact, this paradise is the Face of God, not just an imaginary picture, but the true God Himself. The more the face of our ego fades out, the more the Face of God shines in His Glory, Might, and Goodness. The Desert Path is more a journey within our consciousness than through geographical space and time. That is why it belongs to all people and is not just reserved for desert hermits.

This book will include the following aspects of the journey:

- ➤ the traveler's experiences of the transformation into a Paradise Man in union with God;
- ➤ the traveler's union with fellow humans though still in a challenging world;
- ➤ the traveler's harmonious union with the world of creation in a "cosmic dance." God is the dancer and we are the dance.[6]

The focus of this work will be on "The Paradise Man;" therefore, we will not go into detail about the biography of Thomas Merton and this is not the study about only Merton's theory. We should say that we all enter a mysterious world of Paradise and Thomas Merton is our guide leader. This work is also not aimed as a profound academic research but only a collection of precious notes to help the author himself and other average churchgoers in finding some inspiration for their spiritual journey. "The Paradise Man" will always be the common expression applicable for both "Man" and "Woman."

Biblical citation will be taken from The New American Bible, revised edition.

According to Thomas Merton, you need not be a bishop, a priest, a monk, a nun, a religious or a hermit; you may be a lay person, a normal churchgoer very busy with your daily duties, but you certainly could also be a Paradise Man.

Chapter 1

UNION WITH GOD

1. <u>The Immanent and Transcendent God</u>

Union with God begins by faith in the "immanent" and "transcendent" God; that is to believe in the God Who is everywhere and is acting in everything. However, although God is near, He is still inaccessible to human beings, precisely because of His transcendent nature. Although God is in "paradise," the gap between Him and us is an infinite distance. Human beings cannot reach God by mere human effort. We cannot attain union with Him unless God lowers Himself to reach us, bridging the gap for us. Union with God is by its very nature an act of God's mercy. It is never an achievement of man. Thomas Merton wrote in his meditation in *The Silent Life*:

> **"God, says philosophy, is both immanent and transcendent. By His immanence He lives and acts in the intimate metaphysical depths of everything that exists. He is "everywhere." By His transcendence He is so far above all beings, that no human and limited concept can contain and exhaust His Being. Finite beings are not even said to "be" in the same**

univocal sense. Compared with God, created being "is not;" again, compared with created being, God is not." [7]

Union with God is, therefore, not a superficial mixture, but a very profound action happening in the essence of the true self. It is both an act of contemplation, which is the complete attention of man's whole being toward God's presence and an act of transformation, because to "know" God means also to "become" like Him, to make a change of heart. Thomas Merton defined the union with God:

To be one with One Whom you cannot see, is to be hidden, to be nowhere, to be no one: it is to be unknown as He is unknown, forgotten as He is forgotten, lost as He is lost to the world which nevertheless exists in Him. Yet to live in Him is to live by His power, to reach from end to end of the universe in the might of His wisdom, to rule and form all things in and with Him. It is to be the hidden instrument of His Divine action, the minister of His redemption, the channel of His

mercy, the messenger of His infinite love. [8]

God is, consequently, not only a partner of the union, but He is also the most important cause who has made this union possible.

2. In God, the Self Transforms

In our union with God, there are two important spiritual transformations in the existential structure of the self. The first one is psychological and the second ontological.

The first transformation of the self in reaching the full union with God is the psychological "loss of the self" itself. To make it clearer, it is the loss of self-awareness. According to Merton, this loss is for the greater benefit to the self:

Therefore, as long as we experience ourselves in prayer as an "I" standing on the threshold of the abyss of purity and emptiness that is God, waiting to "receive something" from Him, we are still far from the most intimate and secret unitive knowledge that is pure contemplation... The next step is not

a step. You are not transported from one degree to another. What happens is that the separate entity that is YOU apparently disappears and nothing seems to be left but a pure freedom indistinguishable from infinite freedom. Love identified with Love.[9]

If the entity of "I" apparently disappears in my psyche, I can put total energy and concern and love toward God alone. Thus, I might fulfill the first great commandment:

"You shall love the Lord, your God, with all your heart, with all your soul, and with all your mind. This is the greatest and the first commandment." (Mt 22:37-38)

Thomas Merton called this a "pure love" which could draw the mercy of God and bring peace to the world. He wrote in *New Seeds of Contemplation:*

It is in this ecstasy of pure love that we arrive at a true fulfillment of the First Commandment, loving God with our whole heart and our whole mind

and all our strength. Therefore it is something that all men who desire to please God ought to desire—not for a minute, nor for half an hour, but forever. It is in these souls that peace is established in the world. They are the strength of the world, because they are the tabernacles of God in the world. They are the ones who keep the universe from being destroyed. They are the little ones. They do not know themselves. The whole earth depends on them.[10]

This "self-forgetfulness" was mentioned by St. Teresa of Avila in her *Interior Castle* when she was describing the final stage of the spiritual life, the 7th Mansion:

First, there is a self-forgetfulness which is so complete that it really seems as though the soul no longer existed, because it is such that she has neither knowledge nor remembrance that there is neither heaven nor life nor honor for her, so entirely is she employed in seeking the Honor of

God ... And thus, happens what may, she does not mind in the least, but lives in so strange a state of forgetfulness that, as I say, she seems to no longer have existence ... absolutely none... [11]

This "self-forgetfulness" is, in fact, desired and accepted by the self as a voluntary death in order that God's will be obeyed. Thus, the self joins in the mystery of the Death of Christ so that we might also be Risen with Him. Thomas Merton clearly expressed this truth in his work *He is Risen.*[12]

When the "I" is forgotten, the self is untouchable by "pride," the most subtle and dangerous enemy, which won victory over the strongest spiritual fighters: Lucifer, Adam and Solomon. Merton wrote poetically about any person who chooses to forget the "I":

Here is a man who is dead and buried and gone, and his memory has vanished from the world of man, and he no longer exists among the living who wander about in time: and who will call him proud because the sunlight fills the huge arc of sky over the country where he lived and died

and was buried, back in the days when he existed? [13]

"Pride" is, in fact, only an accidental phenomenon. It cannot stand by itself. Considered philosophically, pride is our enemy. The supposed substance to which all pride belongs is in fact the "I," the illusory ego. When the self reaches the spiritual level of losing self-awareness and the "ego" disappears, the pride also vanishes. Self-forgetfulness is therefore the sign of the death of our inmost enemy because pride **"cannot exist where one is incapable of reflecting on a separate "self" living apart from God."** [14]

This first important spiritual transformation is therefore "the loss of the ego." The ego was born earlier in our life psychologically. In this transformation it is now dead psychologically. When the illusory ego vanishes the Paradise Man lives in the atmosphere of a total freedom. His heart turns back to the innocence and spontaneity of a child, the status of which Jesus said:

> **"Amen, I say to you, unless you turn and become like children, you will not enter the kingdom of heaven."**
> (Matthew 18, 3)

The Paradise Man feels an immense peace and joy. Free from the busyness, fetter and distraction of the false self, the Paradise Man is full of life and ready for a higher change.

The second transformation of the self is an ontological change, and as a change in being, it is the more important event. As was stated above, the true self cannot enter the Kingdom of God by mere human effort. Rather, the Kingdom of God will enter him. Merton wrote:

> **From our side of the threshold of this darkness, it looks deep and vast ... and exciting. There is nothing we can do about entering in. We cannot force our way over the edge, although there is no barrier. But the reason is perhaps that there is also an abyss. There you remain, somehow feeling that the next step will be a plunge, and you will find yourself flying in interstellar space.**[15]

We cannot force our way into the Kingdom of God. Nor does the Kingdom of God invade the human realm, especially into the area of human choice. It happens that the true self voluntarily invites the coming of God into our life with our faith, trust and hope.

In union with God, the indwelling grace of God transforms the self and makes it a New Creation, breathing the new life of the Holy Spirit. This is not superficial change, but rather it is an ontological and substantial change to the degree that St. Paul said: **"I live, no longer I, but Christ lives in me."** (Galatians 2:20)The true self after joining in the death of Christ, rises also with Christ in the risen life. In union with God, the self is united intimately to the degree that we do not think, will and act, but God thinks, wills and acts in us. Merton wrote of this unity:

> **So it is with one who has vanished into God by pure contemplation. God alone is left. He is the "I" Who acts there. He is the One who loves, knows and rejoices ... They are the clean of heart. They see God. He does their will, because His Will is their own. He does all that they want, because He is the One Who desires all their desires. They are the only ones who**

have everything that they can desire. Their freedom is without limit. [16]

This second change of the true self, on the level of being, in the deep union with God is obviously made by an act of God, a movement within God's Kingdom. Merton further developed this in *The New Man:*

> **Ontologically the source of this new life is outside and above ourselves, in God. But spiritually, both the supernatural life and God Himself Who gives it are in the center of our being. He Who is infinitely above us is also within us, and the highest summit of our spiritual and physical life is immersed in His own actuality. If we are only truly real "in Him," it is because He shares His reality with us and makes it our own.** [17]

It is also an ontological change in the reality of the true self which shares in the Incarnation of Christ. By this mystery, the Word of God was incarnate not only in the human nature of Jesus, but also in the whole of humanity. In this way He makes His presence in all men and women of all ages. He made them all one with Him in a "Mystical Body." His resurrection created miraculous effects, He changed the whole humanity into a New Humankind beginning a New Heaven and a New Earth. Thomas Merton described such universal revolution in *The New Man*:

> **Before He died on the Cross, the historical Christ was alone in His human and physical existence. As He Himself said, "unless the grain of wheat fall into the ground and die, it remains alone. But if it die, it brings forth much fruit." [John 12:25] Rising from the death, Jesus lived no longer merely in Himself. He became the vine of which we are the branches. He extends His personality to include each one of us who are united to Him by faith. The new existence which is His by virtue of His resurrection is no longer limited by the exigencies of matter. He can now pass through closed doors, appear in many places at once, or exercise His action upon the**

earth while remaining hidden in the depths of the Godhead: yet these are only secondary aspects of His risen life. The primary aspect of His risen life is His life in the souls of His elect. He is now not only the natural Christ, but the mystical Christ, and as such He includes all of us who believe in Him. As a theologian says: "The natural Christ redeems us, the mystical Christ sanctifies us. The natural Christ died for us, the mystical Christ lives in us. The natural Christ reconciles us to His Father, the mystical Christ unifies us in Him." (Fr. Prat, S.J. –*The Theology of St. Paul*, Westminster, Md., 1952, vol. i, p. 300).[18]

And His Spirit, as the Soul of the whole Mystical Body, blows freely in all parts of the body to sanctify them and to transform them, until they are united fully in Christ, the Incarnated God. Thomas Merton expressed in *The New Man*:

The "new life," the life of the Spirit, life "in Christ," is communicated to the spirit of man by the invisible Mission of

the Holy Spirit—a direct consequence of the Resurrection of Jesus. Therefore the "new creation" instituted by the Second Adam is in fact a prolongation of His Resurrection. The new world which is called the Kingdom of God, the world in which God reigns in man by His divine Spirit . . . [19]

This substantial second transformation of the true self is, therefore, the birth of "the new man." In this new man, humanity shines more as God than as man. Mystics use many beautiful metaphors to express how the self looks when united with God. St. Teresa of Avila used the picture of a white butterfly born from the dead body of a silkworm.[20] Merton used the picture of a crystal which bears a new quality when it is filled with light.[21] No matter what metaphor they used, mystics often confirmed that the self in the state of "union" appears to be more like God than man. St Bernard of Clairvaux gave a description in his book *On The Love of God:*

Just as a little drop of water mixed with a lot of wine seems entirely to lose its own identity, while it takes on the taste of wine and its color; just

as iron, heated and glowing, looks very much like fire, having divested itself of its original and characteristic appearance; just as air flooded with the light of the sun is transformed into the same splendor of light so that it appears not so much lighted up as to be light itself: so it will inevitably happen that in the Saints, every human affection will in some ineffable manner melt away from self and be entirely transfused into the will of God. [22]

3. God: The Paradise

To speak ultimately, those who had the gladness of seeing God and being intimately united with God, enjoyed God as their paradise but they could not describe this experience, because in ecstasy mystics forgot their own experience. Besides, no human language can express the reality of heaven. Merton explained this point:

Would you call this experience? I think you may say that this only

becomes an experience in a man's memory. Otherwise it seems wrong even to speak of it as something that happens. Because things that happen have to happen to some subject, and experiences have to be experienced by someone. But here the subject of any divided or limited or creature experience seems to have vanished. You are not you, you are fruition. If you like, you do not have an experience, you become experience: but that is entirely different, because you no longer exist in such a way that you can reflect on yourself or see yourself having an experience, or judge what is going on . . . And here all adjectives fall to pieces. Words become stupid. Everything you say is misleading . . . unless you list every possible experience and say: "That is not what it is." "That is not what I am talking about." [23]

Mystics, therefore, speak about God only as experience in their memories. An earthly language only manifests relatively some minimum degree of precious experiences about God. With such strict limitation, mystics have expressed God as Being, Life and Love . . .

4. <u>God, the Pure Being</u>

In the Old Testament Moses, after encountering God in the desert, had only a general statement about what God had revealed about Himself: "I AM WHO AM." (Ex. 3:14)

Thomas Merton recalled his own first encountering God as Being through the understanding of Etienne Gilson: God is "**Aseitas;**" that means:

> **"the power of a being to exist absolutely in virtue of itself, not as caused by itself, but as requiring no cause, no other justification for its existence except that its very nature is to exist. There can only be one such Being: that is God."[24]**

God exists as all existing things do, but the difference is that He exists without limit, absolutely, He is Pure Being.

Thomas Merton was shaken by such understanding of God, which enabled him for the first time to accept God and admire Him. This moment made Merton admire Catholic philosophy and later drew him to become a convert. Merton wrote in his autobiography, *The Seven Story Mountain*:

"And the one big concept which I got out of its pages was something that was to revolutionize my whole life." [25]

Day in and day out, Merton meditated and contemplated on The One Who revealed Himself, "I AM WHO AM." This experience of God as Being grew in Merton and prepared him to enter a dialogue with Buddhist Mysticism in the closing years of his life. Merton felt so dear and so close to Buddhist Zen Masters who expressed their Absolute One to be "The Suchness," the Absolute "Ground of Being" in all things.[26]

In studying Teilhard de Chardin, Merton was deeply impressed by the spirituality of this scientific theologian, which begins with love for the gift of existing. He quoted the prayer of Teilhard de Chardin:

O God, Whose call precedes the very first of our movements, grant me the desire to desire being . . . that by means of that divine thirst which is Your Gift, the access to the great waters may open wide within me. Do not deprive me of the sacred taste of being, that primordial energy, that initial point of support: SPIRITU PRINCIPALI CONFIRMA ME. [27]

And Merton comments on Teilhard's prayer:

We should not merely "be" but experience our being in its depths by freely willing to be, by responding to the gift of being that comes to us from God within us, by attaining to a "fontal communion" with Him as the source and center of our life. No finer and more contemplative page has been written in our century. [28]

This Teilhardian mysticism which focuses on "being," "existing," and "being present" is in fact the most appropriate attitude when we approach contemplation, because contemplation is the mindfulness of the presence of God. From the appreciation and gratitude for our being and the world's existence, this spirituality leads us to the appreciation and gratitude for the greatest gift, the presence of God in us and for us. This joy in embracing "being" is the first step toward the extreme joy of embracing the "Being of God," and of uniting with Him. Thomas Merton seems to be right in listing Teilhardian spirituality among the finest contemplative literature of the century in which he lived.

5. <u>The Living God</u>

The Paradise Man enjoys God as Life in three ways:

<u>First, "God is the Center of human life."</u>

He is the ultimate goodness and meaning for the whole human life. Man embraces God tightly as the treasure found in the field. He does not hesitate to sell all things he owns to have enough money to buy that field. (Mt. 13, 44)In *The Waters of Siloe* Thomas Merton wrote of the paradise of those who offer their life to God and have only Him as the fulfillment of life:

Is it not a wonder that Trappist Monasteries are the places full of peace, contentment and joy? These men who have none of the pleasures of the world, have all the happiness the world is unable to find. Their silence is more eloquent than all the speeches of politicians, and the noise of all the radios in America. Their smiles have more joy in them than has the laughter of thousands. When they raise their eyes to the hills or to the sky, they see a beauty which other people do not know how to find. When the monks work in the fields and the forests, they seem to be tired and alone, but their hearts are at rest, and they are absorbed in a companionship that is tremendous, because it is Three Persons in one infinite nature, the One who spoke the Universe and draws it all back into Himself by His Love; the One from Whom all things came and to Whom all things return; and in Whom are all the beauty and

substance and actuality of everything in the world that is real. [29]

The presence of God in human life is more precious than the visit of a noble person or a king. What a privilege that God with His whole dignity as the Alpha and Omega, the origin and fulfillment of the whole universe resides in our hearts. It is when our souls are in union with Him that we are embracing truly the Center of the world. This viewpoint is a very good truth to meditate on when we express gratitude after receiving the Eucharist, or to meditate on the presence of God in our hearts.

When God dwells within us, our hearts become paradises full of God's Glory, and we become tabernacles of God, the bearers of God. Thomas Merton wrote:

> **God Himself dwells in us and we in Him. We are His new paradise. And in the midst of that paradise stands Christ Himself, the Tree of Life. From the base of the tree the four rivers of Eden flow out to irrigate not only all the faculties of our soul and body, filling them with grace and mystical light, but also the whole world around**

us, by the invisible radiation of the Spirit present within us. We are in the world as Christ-bearers and temples of the Holy Spirit, because our souls are filled with His grace. [30]

The living presence of God dwelling in our hearts is not only in regard to holy people, but He is also truly present to sinful people, within their hearts. The Living God, the inner Paradise, is still available at any time to sinners . . . within themselves and waiting for them to enter. That is the teaching of St. Teresa of Avila. [31]

God is present permanently at the center of the self's interior life, the center of our thoughts and wills. Merton murmured in prayer:

God is in this room. So much so, that it is difficult to read or write. Nevertheless I'll get busy on Isaiah which is your Word, O my God, and may your fire grow in me and may I find you in your beautiful fire. It is very quiet, O my God. Your moon shines on our hills. Your moonlight shines in my wide open soul when

everything is silent. Adolezo Peno y muero. [32]

The eyes of God, as Saints have said, in this intimate union keep following you in every step you take and in everything you do. Though they look loving and tender, they are hard to confront when one is not being truthful with others or with oneself. Merton called them the eyes of Truth:

His eyes, which are the eyes of Truth, are fixed upon my heart. Where His glance falls, there is peace; for the light of His Face, which is the Truth, produces truth wherever it shines. . . His eyes are always on us in choir and every where and in all times. No grace comes to us from heaven except He looks upon our hearts. And what is more, He looks at us from within our hearts, for we and He are one. [33]

With the help of God's eyes examining his heart, Merton prays for love:

The trees indeed love you without knowing you. The tiger lilies and corn

flowers are there, proclaiming that they love you, without being aware or Your presence. The beautiful dark clouds ride slowly across the sky musing on You like children who do not know what they are dreaming of, as they play. But in the midst of them all, I know You and I know of Your presence. In them and in me I know of the Love which they do not know, and, what is greater, I am abashed by the presence of Your love in me. O kind and terrible love . . .For in the midst of these beings which have never offended You, I am loved by You, and I would seem most of all as one who has offended You. I am seen by You under the sky, and my offenses have been forgotten by You . . . but I have never forgotten them. Only one thing I ask: that the memory of them should not make me afraid to receive into my heart the gift of Love which You have placed in me. [34]

Second, "God is the Source of Supernatural Life".

That means something much different, as different as heaven and earth. In the first form of union, as expressed above, God, while being our Lover, Mentor, Master and Hero, is basically an "Other" to the self. God, in the second form of union, is on the contrary, "the True Life of the self" in a New Creation. In this New Life, God is Life itself to the self. **"Remain in me, as I remain in you. . . . I am the vine, you are the branches. "** (Jn.15:4-5)

Mystically, the contemplative person sinks into God, the source of Life nourishing all things naturally and supernaturally:

> **Without any need for complicated reasoning or mental efforts or special acts, his life is a prolonged immersion in the rivers of tranquility that flow from God into the whole universe and draw all things back into God. For God's love is like a river springing up in the depth of the Divine Substance and flowing endlessly through His creation, filling all things with life and goodness and strength.** [35]

This Source of Life is Christ, Who is our Resurrection, Who reigns in us and is the Kingdom of God, giving us the citizenship of the new Earth; and Who is also the Son of God holding in us the inheritance of Heaven, enabling us to utter with Him **"Abba, Father!"** (Romans 8: 15) We will get to know more about Christ in the next chapter where we study Christ as the Foundation of the paradise society, the Second Adam.

This Supernatural Life is also the "Life of Grace," which should not be misunderstood as a kind of mysterious substance, a thing, a commodity which is furnished us by God or like fuel for a supernatural engine in order to make our journey to God. It is the presence and action of God Himself within us. Merton wrote in *Life and Holiness:*

> **Grace is not "something with which" we perform good works and attain to God. It is not a "thing" or a "substance" entirely apart from God. It is God's very presence and action within us. Therefore, clearly it is not a commodity we "need to get" from him in order to go to him. For all practical purposes we might as well say that**

grace is the quality of our being that results from the sanctifying energy of God acting dynamically in our life. That is why in the primitive Christian literature, and especially in the New Testament, we read not so much of receiving grace as of receiving the Holy Spirit – God himself. [36]

This Source of Life is therefore the Life of the Holy Spirit Whom Christ breathed into us, "the dulces hospes animas," the "Sweet Guest dwelling in our soul." Merton explained more about Holy Spirit in *Life and Holiness*:

His very presence within us changes us from carnal to spiritual beings (Rom. 8:9), and it is a great pity that we are so little aware of this fact. If we realized the meaning and import of his intimate closeness to us, we would find in him constant joy, strength and peace. We would be more attuned to that secret, inward inclination of the Spirit which is life and peace. (Rom. 8:5) We would be better able to taste and enjoy the fruits of the Spirit. (Gal.

5) We would have confidence in the hidden one who prays within us even when we ourselves are not able to pray well; Who asks for us the things we do not know we need, and who seeks to give us joy we would not dare to seek for ourselves. [37]

Third, "God is Life" means the Mysterious Divine Life of the TRINITY within the self.

The Paradise Man has known God the Son and God the Holy Spirit. In this way of union he will also know God the Father in and through Christ. Jesus said:

"Have I been with you for so long a time and you still do not know me, Philip? Whoever has seen me has seen the Father. How can you say, 'Show us the Father'? Do you not believe that I am in the Father and the Father is in me?" (John 14:9-10)

Merton indicated that the Son, as the "Key of David," opens to the self the deepest and richest treasure of all: **the Mystery of the Father.**

Even the Son is unknown to anyone but the Father. But the Son manifests Himself and His Father in the Holy Spirit Whom He gives to us. The Son, then, by the action of His Grace in our souls, is the "Key of David" of which the liturgy sings in Advent. When His revelation opens our souls, no one can close them. When he closes them, no one can open them again. And He Who alone has power to enter our own dominion, can there unlock an ontological abyss that opens out within us upon the darkness of the Beginning, the Source, the Father.[38]

The self does not only know the Father, he witnesses also the mystery of the Love within the **Trinity**, and he is absorbed into this Divine intimacy and becomes one of the manifestations of **the Love the three Divine Persons give to one another**. Merton wrote his meditation in *Thoughts in Solitude*:

And this is the mystery of our vocation: not that we cease to be men in order to become angels or gods, but

that the love of any man's heart can become God's love for God and man, and my human tears can fall from my eyes as the tears of God because they well up from the motion of His spirit in the heart of His Incarnate Son. [39]

Meister Eckhart expressed the same viewpoint:

"In giving us His love, God has given us the Holy Spirit so that we can love Him with the love wherewith He loves Himself." [40]

6. <u>The Loving God</u>

The Mystery of the Trinity is but the Mystery of Love. Henri Le Saux, O.S.B. gives a great meditation in his small book *Prayer* in which he wrote:

The mystery of God is nothing else than the eternal call of the Father to the Son, the Second Person of the Blessed Trinity: "Thou art My Beloved Son."(Mark 1:11; Ps. 2:7) and the eternal answer of the Son to

the Father: "Abba, Pater. Thou, my Father." (Rom. 8:15; Gal. 4:5), the prayer which was always on the lips of Jesus and in His Heart when He was dwelling as a mortal amongst us mortals, and which He is still addressing to the Father in heaven, the summing up, as it were, of his love, his sacrifice, and of his unending intercession.[41]

And Henri Le Saux explains how Jesus unites our prayer with His, for to pray is to let our True Life, which is the indwelling of Christ within us, fulfill His love of a Son toward His Father and be united with Him:

To pray without ceasing is not so much consciously to think of God, as to act consciously under the guidance of the Spirit; it is to live and act "in Christ" (Gal. 2:20) or rather, to allow Jesus to live freely in us his life as Son of God. It is to be attentive to the Father who comes to us by any path he may choose. It is to hear in all creatures and every event the call

which comes to us from the eternity of God, the Thou which the Father addresses mysteriously to each one of us within the Thou..."Thou art my beloved Son"... by which He calls his Son and pours out his love upon Him. It is to answer with Christ in the Holy Spirit, "Abba, Father," out of the love of our hearts in every act of our conscious life.[42]

Thomas Merton certainly prayed well, in the way Le Saux has pointed out, as when he said the following prayer to the Father:

My Father, I know that you have called me to live alone with You, and to learn that if I were not a mere human, a mere human being capable of all mistakes and all evil, also capable of a frail and errant human affection for You, I would not be capable of being your son. You desire the love of a man's heart because your Divine Son also loves You with a man's heart, and He became man in order that my heart and His Heart should love You in one

love, which is a human love born and moved by Your Holy Spirit.[43]

The above explanation denotes the two substantial spiritual transformations of the self in union with God. The first one is the loss of self-awareness which we call the psychological transformation. In the second transformation, which we call ontological, the Paradise Man does not love God by his natural love, but by the New Love which is the absolute Love of Christ toward His Father. At the moment of "ecstasy," there seems to be only the presence of the Father and the Son loving each other. After that moment when the self comes back to the level of being conscious of himself, he is still marked in memory by the infinite love of this Divine Lover. His happiness on earth seems then only to be these moments of experiencing the Divine Union. His love for God grows tremendously and nothing else on earth seems to have any value to attract him anymore.

St Paul's love of God, which had grown from his experiences of being loved steadfastly by Lord Jesus, gave him strength in passing through every kind of distress:

What will separate us from the love of Christ? Will anguish, or distress, or persecution, or famine, or nakedness, or peril, or the sword? As it is written:"For your sake we are being slain all the day; we are looked upon as sheep to be slaughtered." No, in all these things we conquer overwhelmingly through him who loved us. For I am convinced that neither death, nor life, nor angels, nor principalities, nor present things, nor future things, nor powers, nor height, nor depth, nor any other creature will be able to separate us from the love of God in Christ Jesus our Lord. (Romans 8:35-39)

St Teresa of Avila wrote of the love-sickness of spiritual lovers who have known God once and afterwards nothing on earth could console them for the absence of their God.[44]

Similarly, Merton found the rebellion of William Blake to be a kind of rebellion of God-lovers:

It was the rebellion of the Lover of the Living God, the rebellion of one

**whose desire of God was so intense
and irresistible, that it condemned,
with all its might, all the hypocrisy
and petty sensuality and skepticism
and materialism which cold and trivial
minds set up as impassable barriers
between God and the souls of men.** [45]

If God is Being, if He is Life, if He is Love, what
else better can we say than that God is all to man,
and He Himself is the true Paradise on Earth? In
union with God, saints have lost all fear, anxiety,
self-concern, self-desire and self-plan . . . the first
happiness of a true life is a true peace. It has been
said that when Saint Anthony lived in the desert his
face:

**. . . shone with the simplicity of
peace of Eden and the first days of the
unspoiled world. It was the face that
would make expressions like "self-
possession" and "self-control" look
ridiculous, because here was as man
who was possessed, not by himself,
but by the very Uncreated, Infinite
Peace in Whom all life and all being
lie cradled for eternity.** [46]

Chapter 2

UNION WITH THE WORLD

1. <u>The World is a Paradise</u>

All things in the world, with God's Mighty Presence in the adoring eye of the soul, have changed into a paradise garden. Merton wrote:

> **The only true joy on earth is to escape from the prison of our false self, and enter by love into union with the Life Who dwells and sings within the essence of every creature and in the core of our own souls. In His Love we possess all things and enjoy fruition of the world, everything we meet and everything we see and hear and touch, far from defiling, purifies us and plants in us something more of contemplation and of heaven.[47]**

2. <u>The World is a Place for Celebration</u>

That paradise insight or experience about things changes the face of the world. Under the Divine Love of the Holy Spirit, the world is no longer a land of exile, the earth is no longer an alien planet full of danger to man. The world becomes the common place for celebration. Thomas Merton found the innocent joy of the citizens of the early Mayan cities in Guatemala, and of the Zapotecan city of Monte Alban in Mexico, the exemplary attitude for all citizens of the earth. In *Love and Living*, Merton described these ancient places:

When the Mayan pyramids were first built, the people came together in the great open spaces between the buildings. They were dressed in the most beautiful clothes the world has ever seen, made of the bright feathers of paradise birds. They danced and played a ball game that was also a form of worship, uniting game and ritual. There were as yet no bloody sacrifices (human sacrifices came later with the Toltecs and Aztecs, and military empires).

The first cities of America were spaces marked out for the ample expansion of celebration, joy, worship, play, praise! In the space of celebration built by the people themselves, they

came together in joy, in beauty, and each recognized the other as a fellow creator of common celebration. Their city came alive!

The streets of those cities were not streets in which they watched somebody else going someplace else, where all the joy was hidden behind expensive walls. The streets were places where everyone sang together, converging upon the central dance which was the life and identity of the city. [48]

And Merton expressed with enthusiasm what came to be a common celebration in what we may call a "paradise city." He wrote:

It is the creation of a common identity, a common consciousness. Celebration is everybody making joy. Not as a duty (you can't manufacture joy out of the duty to have fun). Celebration is when we let joy make itself out of love.

We like to dance together.

We like to make pretty and amusing things.

We like to laugh at what we have made.

We like to put bright color on the walls, more bright colors on ourselves.

We like our pictures, they are crazy. Celebration is crazy: the craziness of not submitting, even though "they," "the others," the ones who make life impossible seem to have all the power. Celebration is the beginning of confidence, therefore of power. When we laugh at them, when we celebrate, when we make our lives beautiful, when we give one another joy by loving, by sharing, when we manifest a power they cannot touch, we can be the artisans of a joy they never imagine. . . One day you'll see.[49]

3. <u>The World is Lovely</u>

Thomas Merton told a story of his own about how he looked at the world. At the time he ran away from the world full of turmoil and conflict and hid himself under the roof of the Gethsemani Monastery, he had a great contempt and hatred of the world. However, since he began to learn how to love, he started wrestling with the question: "Is 'the world' a problem?" Seven years later, he came back to the secular world for the first time doing clerical assistance to a Vicar General of his order. He was reconciled with the world, and pointed out that the world with God within it looked much different. He wrote:

> **I went through the city, realizing for the first time in my life how good are all the people in the world and how much value they are in the sight of God.** [50]

Falling in love again with the world, Merton found it very interesting. W. H. Ferry, a friend of Merton, who had seen Merton while on his way to Asia, remembers his excitement, **"He was like a kid going to the circus."**

Merton did have a great love for the world around him. He did not hesitate to say that he wanted to marry the natural world in his hermitage life. He wrote:

> **One might say I had decided to marry the silence of the forest. The sweet dark warmth of the whole world will have to be my wife. Out of the heart of that dark warmth comes the secret that is heard only in silence, but is the root of all the secrets that are whispered by all the lovers in their beds all over the world.** [51]

The world is so lovely that Dostoevski in his book *The Brothers Karamazov* left a legacy to human society through the saintly monk Zosima speaking to his congregation:

> **Love all God's creation, the whole of it and every grain of sand. Love every leaf, every ray of God's light! Love the animals, love the plants, love everything. If you love everything, you will perceive the divine mystery in things. And once you have perceived**

it, you will begin to comprehend it ceaselessly more and more every day. And you will at last come to love the whole world with an abiding, universal love. . . . My friends, ask God for gladness. Be glad as children, as the birds of heaven. Love to fall upon the earth and kiss it. Kiss the earth ceaselessly and love it insatiably. Love all men, love everything, seek that rapture and ecstasy. Water the earth with the tears of your joy and love those tears. [52]

The love for the world makes the Paradise Man more aware of the participation of other beings in his world. Thomas Merton shared with us the world he lived in:

I exist under trees. I walk in the woods out of necessity. I am both a prisoner and an escaped prisoner. I cannot tell you why, born in France, my journey ended here in Kentucky. I have considered going farther, but it is not practical. It makes no difference. Do I have a "day?" Do I spend my

"day" in a "place?" I know there are trees here. I know there are birds here. I know the birds in fact very well, for there are precise pairs of birds (two each of fifteen or twenty species) living in the immediate area of my cabin. I share this particular place with them: we form an ecological balance. This harmony gives the idea of "place" a new configuration.[53]

Not only being more aware of the presence of other things and other people, the Paradise Man could pay more full attention to anyone he meets, anything he sees, and any sound he hears. Being freer from the false self, he could spend more time to listen, to participate, to talk and to share with the creation the life he has in the common world of everything. Let us hear Merton sharing what he heard from the words of a mountain, or Atlas, from his book *Raids on the Unspeakable:*

How lonely is my life as a mountain on the shore of ocean, with my heart at the bottom of the sea and my spirit at the center of the earth where no one can speak to me. I ring my bell

and nobody listens. All I do is look at nothing and change the seasons and hold up the sky and save the world . . . My stability is without fault because I have no connections. I have not viewed mankind for ages. Yet I have not slept, thinking of man and his troubles, which are not alleviated by the change of season . . . I do not tire easily, for this is the work I am used to. Though it is child's play, sometimes I hate it. I bear with loneliness for the sake of man. Yet to be constantly forgotten is more than I can abide.[54]

People often say that when a boy or a girl falling in love sees all things in the world so beautiful, the person wants to sing a song, or become a poet to weave poetic sentences, or be a musician to write thousand of romantic melodies overflowing from the joyful heart. The same and even more happens to the Paradise Man who is now falling in love with God in an extraordinary love. The world of paradise is therefore a world of a mystical romance where the soul searches for God daily as a girl seeks her lover.

King Solomon wrote about such sentiment in *The Song of Songs*:

> **On my bed at night I sought him—whom my soul loves—I sought him but I did not find him. "Let me rise then and go about the city, through the streets and squares; Let me seek him whom my soul loves." I sought him but I did not find him. The watchmen found me, as they made their rounds in the city; "Him whom my soul loves—have you seen him?"- Hardly had I left them. When I found him whom my soul loves, I held him and would not let him go until I had brought him to my mother's house, to the chamber of her who conceived me.** (The Song of Songs, 3:1-4)

4. <u>The World is Immense and Full of Wonders</u>

Let us observe the incredibly vast work of God. Scientists inform us that the Sun is only a medium-sized star in our Milky Way Galaxy and it is 109 times bigger than the Earth, one of its planets. To go to the nearest star we need to travel 4 years and 80 days with the speed of light. The light flies at speed of 186,000 miles or 300,000 kilometers per second. We have just mentioned two stars which are the Sun and its nearest neighbor and they are far from each other over four years for the light to travel. Now, our galaxy, the Milky Way, contains not only few but at least 100 billion stars (www.space.com). If we want to travel across the Milky Way from one side to another, we need to travel by the speed of light for 100,000 years (which means 1,000 centuries or 1,000 human lifetimes). While just alone the Milky Way Galaxy is surprising us with such magnitude, we become indeed tremble in getting to know that the Universe contains 500 hundred billion galaxies (www.dailygalaxy.com). Wow! We cannot imagine how immense the Universe is! Scientists comment that there are more stars in space than grains of sand on all the beaches of the earth. (Universe Today, by Fraser Cain, 2015, Dec 23)

Astronomer Carl Sagan, musing upon the meaning of the Earth in a photo taken by Voyager 1 as it sped out of Solar System about 4 billion miles away from the Earth, wrote in his book *Pale Blue Dot* about the humble existence of the Earth in this immense Universe:

"We succeeded in taking that picture [from deep space], and, if you look at it, you see a dot. That's here. That's home. That's us. On it everyone you know, everyone you love, everyone you've ever heard of, every human being who ever was, lived out their lives, the aggregate of all our joys and sufferings, thousands of confident religions, ideologies and economic doctrines. Every hunter and forager, every hero and coward, every creator and destroyer of civilizations, every king and peasant, every young couple in love, every hopeful child, every mother and father, every inventor and explorer, every teacher of morals, every corrupt politician, every superstar, every supreme leader, every saint and sinner in the history of our species, lived there, on a mote of dust suspended in a sunbeam."[55]

We can hardly believe that the world is so immense. It leads us to another truth: How much more enormous the Creator of such an immense

Universe could be?! People do not often know that God is that great! That is our Creator Who created the universe by His hand with "more stars in space than all the grains of sand on earth". That is our God. The work of creating the earth and everyone of our human race is only a very tiny tiny work of His creativity.

The world is truly vast. That is talking about quantity, how about quality? This topic will make us even more delighted. Each thing in nature is a work of supreme art. You may say that it is a miracle. It is true. Writers, painters and poets have tried to describe the beauty of nature, but their works are just like some rough works of kindergarten children before the accomplishments of the Great Art Master. Anthony de Mello comments in his book *The Song of the Birds*:

> **If you really heard a bird sing, if you really saw a tree . . . you would know beyond words and concepts. What was that you said? That you have heard dozens of birds sing and seen hundreds of trees? Ah, was it the tree you saw or the label? When you look at a tree and see a tree you**

have really not seen the tree. When you look at a tree and see a miracle, then, at least, you have seen the tree! Did your heart ever feel with wordless wonder when you heard the song of a bird? [56]

Thomas Merton confirmed the above point that miraculous realities of paradise only appear when all words and concepts disappear, as in his poem named "The Fall" in *Collected Poems:*

They bear with them in the center of nowhere the unborn flower of nothing:
This is the paradise tree. It must remain unseen until word ends and arguments are silent. [57]

In the paradise world there is never a dull minute because it is ever changing, ever new. When we see a star in the sky, it stays no more in that spot because its light has taken million years to arrive in our eyes while it has been moving across a very remote distance. People said that you could never see the same flowing water in a river. Everything in the world is never the same every moment. Nikos

Kazantzakis gave testimony about Zorba, who had the way of a Paradise Man; he saw everything as though for the first time:

> **He had just what a quill driver needs for deliverance; the primordial glance which seizes its nourishment arrow-like from on high; the creative artlessness, renewed each morning, which enabled him to see all things constantly as though for the first time, and to bequeath virginity to the eternal quotidian elements of air, ocean, fire, woman, and bread; the sureness of hand, freshness of heart, the gallant daring to tease his own soul; finally the savage bubbling laugh from a deep, deep, wellspring, deeper than the bowels of man, a laugh which at critical moments spurted and was able to demolish (did demolish) all the barriers --morality, religion, homeland . . .[58]**

5. <u>The World is Sacred</u>

The Paradise Man is enraptured watching nature not only because of its aesthetic beauty but because of its sacredness. Moses heard God's voice when he was approaching the bush on fire: "**Do not come near! Remove your sandals from your feet, for the place where you stand is holy ground**." (Exodus 3: 5) Thomas Merton found that every place is a holy ground filled with the presence of God. He expressed it in *New Seeds of Contemplation:*

> **A tree gives glory to God by being a tree. For in being what God means it to be it is obeying Him. It "consents" so to speak, to His creative love. It is expressing an idea which is in God and which is not distinct from the essence of God, and therefore the tree imitates God by being a tree. . .**
>
> **The forms and individual characters of living and growing things, of inanimate beings, of animals and flowers and all nature, constitute their holiness in the sight of God. Their inscape is their sanctity. It is**

the imprint of His wisdom and His reality in them. [59]

Thus, the Paradise Man, in paying attention to things in the world, enters into contemplation in which he reveres the sacredness contained in these objects. God pours out His glory in each object of His creation by giving His will, His thoughts, His wisdom, His planning, His love and power. Each object is a treasure holding Divine Sanctity, each object becomes a 'tabernacle' of God. We enjoy a delightful surprise in seeing Merton using metaphor well when he called each natural thing a "saint."

The pale flowers of the dogwood outside this window are saints. The little yellow flowers that nobody notices on the edge of the road are saints looking up into the face of God. This leaf has its own texture, its own pattern of veins and its own holy shape, and the bass and trout hiding in the deep pools of the river are canonized by their beauty and their strength. The lakes hidden among the hills, and the sea, too, is a saint who

praises God without interruption in her majestic dance.[60]

In that spirit of contemplation, the world with its sacredness becomes an almost infinite prayer offered by the Paradise Man. Merton wrote about this state:

> **Let me seek, then, the gift of silence, and poverty, and solitude, where everything I touch is turned to prayer, where the sky is my prayer, the birds are my prayer, the wind in the trees is my prayer, for God is all in all.** [61]

The Paradise Man can pray easily like that because his eyes and his heart not only see things as the works of God, but through them he sees God Himself so clearly. Nature becomes as a window. Merton wrote in *Bread in the Wilderness*:

> **Creation had been given to man as a clean window through which the light of God could shine into men's souls. Sun and moon, night and day, rain, the sea, the crops, the flowering tree, all these things were transparent.**

They spoke to man not of themselves only but of Him who made them. Nature was symbolic. [62]

The long human pilgrimage to seek for a touch of invisible God is expressed by Saint Augustine in his *Confessions:* **"Thou has made us for thyself, O Lord, and our heart is restless till it rests in Thee."** A primordial moment of profound peace and joy in experiencing God' loving presence is sometimes very simple through simple things in nature which God uses in nurturing us such as air, light, water. . . Thomas Merton shared with us one of his paradise experience in *Dancing in the Water of Life*:

Wonderful clear water pouring strongly out of a cleft in the mossy rock. I drank from it in my cupped hands and suddenly realized it was years, perhaps twenty-five or thirty years, since I had tasted such water: absolutely pure and clear, and sweet with the freshness of untouched water, no chemicals!! I looked up at the clear sky and the tops of leafless trees shining in the sun and it was a

moment of angelic lucidity. Said Terce with great joy, overflowing joy, as if the land and woods and spring were all praising God through me. Again their sense of angelic transparency of everything, and of pure, simple and total light. The word that comes closest to pointing to it is simple. It was all simple.[63]

The Paradise Man, standing among all the sacred objects of nature as the high priest, uses his understanding and love as the fire to offer God the sacrifice. Merton wrote in *The New Man*:

If man was the most exalted among bodily things, it was in order that he might contemplate God and praise Him, as the high priest of the universe. Placed at the exact ontological center of creation, a little less than the angels but charged with command over brute and inanimate beings, Adam was the anointed mediator between God and his world, the priest offered all things to God without destroying them or harming them. For the destruction

did not enter the concept of sacrifice until after the fall. It was in the mystical union of Adam's soul with God that the whole world was offered and consecrated to God in sacrifice. It was in the sounding solitude of Adam's understanding that things without reason became able to adore their creator, in the flaming silence of Adam's wisdom all that existed and breathed and grew and ran and multiplied upon the earth was united with God in worship and in communion. [64]

Later Jesus, true God and true man, is the Most High Priest, the One Mediator. Jesus even performed the most important sacrifice in the history of the universe by offering His own blood to obtain salvation for all humans. (Heb 7:26-28)

Not only man in the midst of nature prays to God, creatures in nature also pray with him. That is the point expressed by author Dostoevski in his book *The Brothers Karamazov* through the saintly character Zosima:

It was a warm, bright, still July night. The river was broad, a mist was rising from it and from time to time we could hear the soft splash of a fish. The birds were silent. All was still and beautiful, all was praying to God. Only we two were not asleep, the peasant lad and I, and we began to talk of the beauty of God's world and the great mystery of it. Every blade of grass, every small insect, ant, golden bee, all of them knew so marvelously their path, and without possessing the faculty of reason, bore witness to the mystery of God, constantly partaking in it themselves. . . . .the world is for all; all creation, all creatures, every leaf are striving towards the Lord, glorify the Lord, weep to Christ, and unknown to themselves, accomplish this by the mystery of their sinless life. [65]

6. <u>Work in Paradise</u>

When approaching things with peace and love because of the presence of God, with respect and reverence because of their sacredness, the work of Paradise Man is an act of worship. He reaches them not for any attempted exploitation, but to celebrate, to pay homage to God, and to show Him his love. Merton wrote in *The New Man*:

> **Adam's work was worship. The work of those who work because they are driven by passion and cupidity is not worship but struggle, not freedom but (psychological) compulsion. If our work is to become contemplative, we must be free enough from things to be able to respect them instead of merely exploiting them. We must not only use them, but value their use, and appreciate them justly for what they are ... In a word our work ought to be a dialogue with reality and therefore a conversation with God.** [66]

In working, the Paradise Man aims at some purpose, but in union with God. He does not feel anxiety and agitation as if he alone did the tasks. He trusts in God and lets Him bring any result He wants. With such a spirit he does his various works with complete emptiness and makes them real acts of worship, rather than acts to exalt the ego. Merton wrote in *No Man Is An Island*:

> **It gives great glory to God for a person to live in this world using and appreciating the good things of life without care, without anxiety, and without inordinate passion. In order to know and love God through His gifts, we have to use them as if we used them not (I Cor. 7:31) . . . and yet we have to use them. For to use things as if we used them not means to use them without selfishness, without fear, without afterthought, and with perfect gratitude and confidence and love of God.** [67]

7. Creativity in Paradise

In creating things, the Paradise Man acts in this same way, but to an even greater degree. Thomas

Merton, in speaking of a true attitude for an artist in the modern world quoted the words of Daisetz Suzuki, which he considered to be adequate:

"The artist, at the moment when his creativeness is at its height, is transformed into an agent of the Creator."[68]

In the same essay, the reality of artists as "the agents of the Creator" was made even more manifest in the dance of the Balinese, in reference to which Merton wrote in *The Literary Essays of T.M.*:

Speaking of Balinese Dancers, Ananda Coomaraswamy alludes to their essentially passive and 'limp' attitude, which enables them to respond to the will of an invisible master who, so to speak, moves them in the sacred dance.[69]

Therefore, any artistic work of the Paradise Man is, in fact, not his own work, but the melding of his own work with the heavenly artistry of God.

Thomas Merton presented the theology of creativity in the same essay. He recalled the work of

Adam in the paradise before the Fall as the privilege to be given a share in the creativity of God. That privilege is still active because the creativity of God still continues. He wrote:

The creative will of God has been at work in the cosmos since He said: "Let there be light." This creative *fiat* was not uttered merely at the dawn of time. All time and all history are a continued, uninterrupted creative act, a stupendous, ineffable mystery in which God has signified his will to associate man with himself in his work of creation. [70]

The participation of humankind in the creativity of God is not only the activity of artists but of all people who are the off-spring of Adam and Eve. Considering the context of the Paradise which was lost and regained, the human creative participation of the Paradise Man today is the involvement in the redemption of his own kind and the restoration of the cosmos, purified and transfigured, to God the Father, the recapitulation of all things for the Eschatological Event.

The creative Christian is not a special kind of Christian, but every Christian has his own creative work to do, his own part in the mystery of the New Creation. [71]

Chapter 3

UNION WITH HUMANKIND

In this chapter we will find the Paradise Man in relationship with his fellow humans, how he treats them and especially how he faces evils in human world; and finally his joy and honor in meeting the most interesting Paradise Man who is the Second Adam.

1. <u>Unity in Humankind</u>

The Paradise Man with the eyes of an innocent child finds everything in nature a gift from God, full of wonder and sanctity. However among the whole creation a human being is even more precious because each one has not only a beautiful body but the spirit inside which is the most mysterious. Though being still a child, boy or girl, a human being has intelligence, free will, and the way of his heart. That is why among all bodily creatures God loves humans the most because they have the image of God. Each person is a miraculous being, a live novel. Therefore, the Paradise Man feels a deep appreciation for the presence of everyone on the earth no matter who they are, what they do, what color of skin they have, what language they speak, or what age is moderating the speed of their actions. The other is not a "hell" as the philosopher

Jean-Paul Sartre said in his play *No Exit*, [72] but a "true paradise" embracing miraculous treasures. Thomas Merton reflected on the variety of his brother monks in the monastery:

> It is very quiet. I think about this monastery that I am in. I think about the monks, my brothers, my fathers. These are the ones who have a thousand things to do. Some are busy with food, some with clothing, some with fixing the roof. Some paint the house, some sweep the rooms, some mop the floors of the refectory. One goes to the bees with a mask on and takes away their honey. Three or four others sit in a room with typewriters and all day long they answer the letters of the people who write here asking for prayers because they are unhappy. Still others are fixing tractors and trucks, others are driving them. The brothers are fighting the mules to get them into harness. Or they go out in the pasture after the cows. Or they worry about the rabbits. One of them

says he can fix watches. Another is making plans for the monastery in Utah. The ones who have no special responsibility for chickens or pigs, or writing pamphlets or packing them up to send out by mail, or keeping the complicated accounts in our Mass book --the ones who have nothing special to do, can always go out and weed the potatoes and hoe the rows of corn. . . Congregavit nos in unum Christi amor. [73]

"Congregavit nos in unum Christi amor" means the love of Christ congregated us in one. Daisetz Suzuki, the Zen scholar and friend of Merton, was asked about "others." He thought a moment and then answered: **"There are no others."**[74] This scholar understood the same truth which Jesus Christ taught his disciples concerning the great commandment, **"You shall love your neighbor as yourself."** (Mt. 22:39)

Jesus, in fact, taught his disciples a much higher charity when He prayed for their unity: **"I pray. . . . so that they may all be one, as you, Father, are in me and I in you"** (Jn.17:21). **"Holy Father, keep**

them in your name that you have given me, so that they may be one just as we are." (Jn. 17:11). How could mankind reach the level of unity in God the Trinity, the unity which makes the three Divine Persons an absolute oneness? This unity which Jesus prayed for in His disciples is realized in its perfection only in the love of the Three Persons of the Holy Trinity for One Another flowing in and through humankind.

Carrying the oneness of the Trinity, humankind is one in all dimensions. The spiritual life of each person is not a private affair but a share in the spiritual life of the Communion of Saints. Merton found an excellent paradise sample in Gandhi, a Hindu holy man, who lived in recent times:

> **This, then, is [a] crucial principle that we discover in Gandhi. Contrary to what has been thought in recent centuries in the West, the spiritual and interior life in not an exclusively private affair. (In reality, the deepest and most authentic Western traditions are at one with those of the East on this point). The spiritual life of one person**

is simply the life of all manifesting itself in him. [75]

Thomas Merton applied the same point in ascetical practices and emphasized that all these pious activities are not only for the individual's benefit, but also contribute to the communal sanctity in which each person partakes. Merton wrote of this unity in *No Man is an Island:*

Every other man is a piece of myself, for I am part and a member of mankind. Every Christian is a part of my own body, because we are members of Christ. What I do is also done for them and with them and by them. But each one of us remains responsible for his own share in the life of the whole body. Charity cannot be what it is supposed to be as long as I do not see that my life represents my own allotment in the life of a whole supernatural organism to which I belong. Only when this truth is absolutely central do other doctrines fit into their proper context. Solitude, humility, self-denial, action

and contemplation, the sacraments, the monastic life, the family, war and peace --none of these make sense, except in relation to the central reality which is God's Love living and acting in those whom He has incorporated in His Christ. Nothing at all makes sense, unless we admit, with John Donne, that: "No man is an island; every man is a piece of the continent, a part of the main." [76]

The concept of "No man is an island" could be accepted more easily when we compare it with the activity of various parts in our physical body. Each part has a distinguished function to do, but the benefit is for the whole body. The legs should not tell the mouth that: "I envy you for your task because you enjoy good food from many cuisines;" but the mouth replies: "Well, my job is truly to enjoy as much good food as possible, but I do this not for myself but for the nutrition and the healthy life of all members in the whole body." The nose should not tell the legs: "You legs are really the luckiest parts in the body. You enjoy walking to many places, you even get privilege in traveling in many remote cities and well known spots!" but the legs reply: "Well, we do not go for just the joy of the legs, but for the good of the whole body. If we do not go, the body could not get to dining room to eat, nor to church to pray, nor to school to study, nor to the company to work. Just as the heart keeps beating day and night surely not for her own fun but for the circulation of oxygen and nutrition to every part of the body." Thus each human being is, though individual, various in talent, different in thought and will, having a separate work to do, a personal life to live, yet he is always also an integral part of the whole humankind and lives for the happiness of all. Saint Paul expressed the same thought in the *First Letter of Corinthians*:

> **"As a body is one though it has many parts, and all the parts of the body, though many, are one body, so also Christ. For in one Spirit we were all baptized into one body, whether Jews or Greeks, slaves or free persons, and we were all given to drink of one Spirit."** (1Cor: 12: 12-13)

2. <u>Disinterested Love: The Main Activity</u>

In this paradise of humankind there is only one activity, which is performed in many different services. That activity is Love, the "beatitude of heaven." [77] The standard is a "disinterested love," a love which is gratuitous, given simply and freely without any condition, without any reason of laws, duty, without any benefit received in return. A disinterested love is also exchanged among the "citizens of paradise" in the state of self-forgetfulness. Thomas Merton wrote about this "standard" love:

A monastery is supposed to be a "school of charity" (i.e. disinterested love), a school of *agape* rather than *eros*. Disinterested love is also called the "love of friendship," that is to say a love which rests in the good of the beloved, not in one's own interest or satisfaction, not in one's own pleasure. A love which does not exploit, manipulate, even by "serving," but which simply loves. A love which in the words of St Bernard, "loves because it loves" and for no other reason or purpose, is therefore "perfectly free."[78]

By loving each other on earth, human beings reflect most perfectly the image of God in them, because the main activity in the Godhead is also the Divine Love among Persons of the Holy Trinity.

"Disinterested love" directed by an egoless heart brings following effects:

- First, disinterested love liberates those who are loved.

It is not possessive and it does not capture or imprison anyone. This real love provides caring and kindness and still lets the loved one feel peaceful. It makes one feel at home, at ease, not owned or restrained. Thomas Merton once gave the example of this kind of supernatural love in the lives of the Privats, a peasant couple, who lived in the farm land of Murat, Auvergne, France.[79] Such love contributes to the paradise atmosphere.

- Secondly, this disinterested love nourishes the loved ones, gives them opportunity to grow, allowing room for them to become more spiritually mature. This opportunity to grow especially reveals itself when such love is fully reciprocal. Merton wrote:

In the mystery of social love there is found the realization of "the other" not only as one to be loved by us, so that we may perfect ourselves, but also as one who can become more perfect by loving us. The vocation to charity is a call not only to love but to be loved. [80]

- Thirdly, the disinterested self, originating in the "truth of human finitude," pours out a gentle compassion toward other finite human beings, and a reverence towards God's Mercy. Concerning this, Merton referenced St Bernard's "three degrees of truth" in his book *The Waters of Siloe*:

The first truth is that of the self. Man, when seeing his own finitude, human weakness and insufficiency, becomes self-forgetful, "enjoying" a life of freedom from self-care. His acceptance of this truth about himself protects him from the temptation to try to be his own god, which our first parents encountered in the first paradise.

The second truth is that of others. Man, knowing his own finitude, becomes deeply compassionate towards the weakness and failures of other human beings. The more he is true to this truth, the more he has a "gentle love" towards others. He walks in the world of imperfection with a great "gentleness" (spiritus lenitatus). [81]

The third truth is the truth of God. Nobody sees the truth of human finitude as clearly as God. Therefore, the man of truth is able to feel the compassion and gentle love of God, which is poured fully into this world, on the Paradise Man and all others. Paradise is, therefore, the land of freedom from self, the "Land of Gentle Love."

- Fourthly, disinterested love is concrete. Not only Christians know the value of Love, for almost all religions teach about "Love." Merton recalled that once, when he had visited his old friend Suzuki, he was surprised and impressed profoundly by the farewell word of his friend: "The most important thing is Love." [82]

Non-religious humanists such as Albert Camus and others have known well the value of love, too. Camus wrote in his *Notebooks*:

If someone here told me to write a book on morality, it would have a hundred pages and ninety-nine would

be blank. On the last page I should write, 'I recognize only one duty that is to love'. And as far as everything else is concerned, I say NO.[83]

Concerning "love," the belief of non-Christians and atheists challenge Christianity regarding the real value of its charity in concrete actions.

Paradise love, considered as real Christian Charity, was taught and repeated many times by Merton.[84] Merton recalled the teaching of Jesus, **""The sabbath was made for man, not man for the sabbath."** (Mark 2:27) and of St. James, **"Religion that is pure and undefiled before God and the Father is this: to care for orphans and widows - in their affliction and to keep oneself unstained by the world..."** (James 1:27) Disinterested love, proper to "Paradise," was therefore expressed by Merton as **"the involvement in one another's history."**[85] This "involvement" in others' history within a suffering world is the communal task of the whole "Mystical Body of Christ," working towards a new future, the fullness of the Kingdom of God.[86]

3. <u>Paradise in a Suffering World</u>

While studying about "paradise," we cannot forget the mystery and reality of evil in a suffering world, which exists in a thousand forms of pain, both physical and mental. This suffering world exists, in fact, as a paradox, a challenge, a denial of the Kingdom of God.

a. <u>The sign of true hope.</u>

Paradise appears, however, as an "emblem of hope." Fortunately, as we will see, the more that human beings fall to the bottom of desperation, the more they are purified from false hopes, false promises, and the more they have a chance to see the true face of the "eternal hope."

A Paradise Man is one, who is able to see his hope in darkness, and his joy in the gravest pain. Merton wrote in *New Seeds of Contemplation:*

> **Yet, strangely, it is in this helplessness that we come upon the beginning of joy. We discover that as long as we stay still, the pain is not so bad and there is even a certain peace, a certain richness, a certain strength,**

a certain companionship that makes itself present to us when we are beaten down and lie flat with our mouths in the dust, hoping for hope.[87]

A hope which exists in the most desperate circumstances is a "surprising" thing to everyone. In reading Starets Zosima 's words, "We do not understand that life is paradise, for it suffices only to wish to understand, and at once paradise will appear in front of us in its beauty," Merton commented:

Taken in the context of the Brothers Karamazov, against the background of violence, blasphemy and murder which fill the book, this is indeed an astonishing statement.[88]

b. The new dimension of suffering.

How could a saint enjoy his "paradise" when people around him are dying from hunger, illness, loneliness, madness, coldness? How could a paradise person remain "peaceful" while other human beings are in anguish by the fear of war and destruction? How could a saint find his paradise within a world suffering from so many evils? These questions can be answered if we know the attitude of the saints. They awake in us a new understanding of evil and suffering.

The essence of suffering is the manifestation of human finitude, either considered as the ability to receive pain or the ability to create pain for others. That is the truth of natural yet fallen humanity in its wounded limitation.

If it is the truth, then the only proper attitude is to admit it, not to deny it or falsify it. All saints have enough humility to accept the truth of their own fallen humanity. Merton wrote that man should recognize and accept the status of his "nothingness:"

> **What does it mean to know and experience my own "nothingness?" It is not enough to turn away in disgust from my illusions, faults and mistakes, to separate myself from them as if they were not, and as if I was someone other than myself. This kind of self-annihilation is only a worse illusion, it is a pretended humility which, by saying "I am nothing," I mean in effect "I wish I were not what I am." This**

**can flow from an experience of our
deficiencies and of our helplessness,
but it does not produce any peace in
us. To really know our "nothingness"
we must also love it. And we cannot
see that it is good unless we accept it.** [89]

Now comes the central question: What good
is our "nothingness," "helplessness," "fallen
woundedness," "limitedness?"

The answer is **"our helplessness, even our
spiritual or moral misery, attracts to us the mercy
of God."** [90] Though man does not have anything of
his own, he has the "mercy of God" within Christ's
Paschal Mystery, which is the source of all good.
The more misery a Paradise Man might be caught
in, the richer the treasure of the mercy of God and the
greater share in Christ's Paschal Mystery he knows
he has. That is the secret of paradise in bottom of
a suffering world. Thomas Merton prayed to God:

**That you perhaps have no greater
"consolation" (if I may so speak) than
to console Your afflicted children
and those who came to You poor and
empty handed with nothing but their**

humanness and their limitations and great trust in Your mercy...

You who do not wait for me to become great before You will be with me and hear me and answer me. It is my lowliness and humanness that have drawn You to make me Your equal by condescending to my level and living in me by Your merciful care.[91]

The Desert Path is the process of the purification of man's soul from all false hopes and empty promises of the world, especially the false hope in mere human effort, the vain promises of human abilities, which all fall short in death. The desert, within the Paschal Mystery, is in fact as wide as all sufferings in the world, and as deep as any level of pain a person might face interiorly. The desert should also be understood to be any kind of limitedness of the world.

In the journey of this vast desert of life, man cannot trust in himself, he cannot depend on his own strength, his only hope is in the mercy of God. The life of a Paradise Man in the midst of evil and a suffering world is, therefore, nothing but the life of "depending on God completely," and having God as the only joy of life. A psalmist wrote this heart's feeling in the psalm 91 as following:

> **You who dwell in the shelter of the Most High, who abide in the shade of the Almighty, say to the Lord, "My refuge and fortress, my God in whom I trust." He will rescue you from the fowler's snare, from the destroying plague, He will shelter you with his pinions, and under his wings you may take refuge; his faithfulness is a protecting shield. You shall not fear the terror of the night nor the arrow that flies by day, nor the pestilence that roams in darkness, nor the plague that ravages at noon.** (Ps 91: 1-6)

Evil and the "suffering world" do not consequently constitute a "problem" anymore. No saint is afraid of "sufferings." The "suffering world" provides the "door" to enter paradise, and the "key" of true happiness. Sufferings become something ordinary, a door that everyone has to pass through to reach the greater value of life. Thomas Merton wrote:

Suffering is not a "problem" as if it were something we could stand outside of and control. Suffering as both Christianity and Buddhism see, each in its own way, is part of our very ego-identity and empirical existence, and the only thing to do about it is to plunge right into the middle of contradiction and confusion in order to be transformed by what Zen calls the "Great Death" and Christianity calls "Dying and Rising with Christ." [92]

The life of a saint is nothing but continuously immersing himself in this death in order to rise continuously with Christ in the new Life. "Dying" therefore is a normal task which the Paradise Man does daily, and often in order to "Rise" daily. Saints, as they live the Paschal Mystery, become detached from subordinate values as joy or suffering, earth or heaven, etc. Johu, an enlightened man of Zen Buddhism, expressed the same idea:

"Pray that all beings may be born in paradise, but as to myself, let me forever remain in this ocean of tribulations." [93]

The Paradise Man does not complain of any tribulation or hardship which comes to his life, but joyfully waits for the mercy of God and accepts any manifestation of His Providence. At the closing of *Seven Storey Mountain*, Merton wrote down his last meditation, which was a concluding dialogue between God and his soul. God said:

> **But you shall taste the true solitude of my anguish and my poverty and I shall lead you into the high places of my Joy and you shall die in Me and find all things in My mercy, which has created you for this end, and brought you from Prades to Bermuda to St. Antonin to Oakham to London to Cambridge to Rome to New York to Colombia to Corpus Christi to St. Bonaventure to the Cistercian Abbey of the poor men who labor in Gethsemani: that you may become the brother of God and learn to know the Christ of burnt men.** [94]

c. Unity of the paradise and the suffering world

Paradise is, however, not a passive, quiescent life with selfish satisfaction and comfort for paradise persons. Since there is no longer "ego" in paradise, there is not a single Paradise Person who lives for himself. For paradise is the life in union with God in Christ. (However, there still is the serpent lurking in paradise!) As long as Christ is still undergoing trials with the rest of His Mystical Body, the Paradise Man joins in the same suffering in order to rise in the same resurrection with Christ. (Romans 8:14-17) Thomas Merton expressed metaphorically the unity of Christ with His members in the violent world in his work *New Seeds of Contemplation:*

> **"Christ is massacred in His members, torn limb from limb; God is murdered in men."**[95]

Chapter 9 in the Acts of the Apostles tells the story of the conversion of Saint Paul who was on the way to Damascus to arrest followers of Christ and got struck by the Lord. In the flask of a light he fell off his horse and heard a voice saying to him, "Saul, Saul, why are you persecuting me?" He said, "Who are you, sir?" The reply came, "I am Jesus, whom you are persecuting. (Acts 9: 1-5) The conversation confirmed this belief in the Mystical Body of Christ who is present in all believers and bears sufferings with them.

By the nature of the "Mystical Body" to which the paradise man belongs, he is still undergoing trial as long as there is still another single human person left in the world of alienation, torture, oppression, murder, hunger, loneliness, and in the struggle of choice between truth and falsity, good and evil, death and life. Jesus Christ was resurrected, but His Mystical Body has not fully been resurrected yet. Christ is still waiting for this fulfillment. The angel said to the women: **"Then go quickly and tell his disciples, 'He has been raised from the dead, and he is going before you to Galilee; there you will see him."** (Matthew 28:7) To meet Christ and to unite with Him, the Paradise Man does not seek for Him in heaven, but in the world of struggling people where Christ is going ahead of him in history and helping other members of His to "break through" (the crucial moment of spiritual transformation as expressed by Meister Eckhart), [96] which is to dare to die in order to rise again into the New Life. Meeting Christ at a crucial moment in the life of another means getting involved in their life.[97]

The nature of the "unity" in the "Mystical Body" reveals the life of a Paradise Person as "extremely active," for he cannot be at rest as long as a single member of humanity is still in pain spiritually or physically.

The suffering world being transformed into Paradise was biblically pictured as a mother who is in pain giving birth to her child. (Apocalypse 12:2; John 16: 20-22; Romans 8:22, 23) The pain remains until the whole body of the child with all his members is delivered from evil and suffering and emerges to see the paradise world. The Paradise Man, therefore, is still joining Christ in being born again and again in every member of Christ until the end the world.

4. <u>Paradise Apostolate</u>

There are many ways of apostolate and of social action in the suffering world. The simplest and most effective way is to "witness." The Paradise Man gives the strongest message to others by revealing his status of "paradise life." Thomas Merton recalled his experience of seeing a black woman who shined out through her eyes a "deep, deep, unfathomable, shining peace." This woman of Harlem, the poor slum of New York, existed there, by the Providence of God, obviously not only "to receive" support but to "give" it:

Living in the same building as most of the Friendship House workers was an aging Negro woman, thin, quiet, worn out, dying of cancer... The only time I spoke to her and got a good look at her, I realized one thing: she possessed the secret of Harlem, she knew the way out of the labyrinth. For her, the paradox had ceased to exist, she was no longer in the cauldron, except by the pure accident of physical presence which counts for nothing, for the cauldron is almost entirely of the moral order. And when I saw her and spoke to her, I saw in this tired, serene, and holy face the patience and joy of the martyrs and the clear, unquenchable light of sanctity. She and some other Catholic women were sitting in chairs by the doorsteps of the building, in the relatively cool street, in the early evening: and the

group they made, there, in the midst of the turmoil of the lost crowd, astounded the passerby with the sense of peace, of conquest: that deep, deep, unfathomable, shining peace that is the eyes of Negro women who are really full of belief.[98]

That "astounding peace" is not the private possession of special people but it could belong to anyone who has the secret of paradise, which is to "distrust" your own wisdom and to "trust" in "God's mercy." Thomas Merton told of the experience of this "paradise peace," which came to him once when he was confused in the midst of the process of being drafted for military duty, when he was taking a ride in the countryside:

The country opened out before us . . . My eyes opened and took all this in. And for the first time in my life I realized that I no longer cared whether I preserved my place in all this or lost it: whether I stayed here or went to the army. All that no longer mattered. It was in the hands of One Who loved me far better than I could

ever love myself: and my heart was filled with peace.

It was the peace that did not depend on houses, or jobs, or places, or times, or external conditions. It was the peace that time and material created situations could never give. It was peace that the world could not give. [99]

The apostolate of the spirit of "witnessing" is of course not the agitation of exterior activism or the show of a "distinguished ego." On the contrary, it is the fruit of a true interior life, it is the tree cultivated by the spirit of "self-forgetfulness" and watered by a "disinterested love." With respect to this, Thomas Merton offers a recommendation:

Try to make your activity bear fruit in the same emptiness and silence and detachment you have found in contemplation. Ultimately, the secret of all this is perfect abandonment to the will of God . . . If you do this, your activity will share the disinterested peace that you are able to find at prayer, and in the simplicity of things you do,

**men will recognize your peacefulness
and will give glory to God.** [100]

In the interior life, the Love of God is central. Thomas Merton indicated that the real apostolate does not come from the "quantity" of external works such as rosaries, masses, prayers, fasting, but from the "quality" of the love and union with God. [101]

Above all, it is not the natural and human love of the Paradise Man that could inflame the whole world, but the Divine Love of God that could transform the world into His Kingdom. The Paradise Man, therefore, does not sanctify the world by his own piety and holiness, or by his ability to preach and argue, but by God Himself. Merton quotes the teaching of St. John of the Cross on this point. Yet says Merton if this sublime fire of infused love burns in your soul, it will inevitably send forth throughout the church and the world an influence more tremendous than could be estimated by the radius reached by words or by example. Saint John of the Cross writes:

**"A very little of this pure love is
more precious in the sight of God and
of greater profit to the Church, even
though the soul appears to be doing**

nothing, than are all other works put together." [102]

The essential duty of the Paradise Man is not to hinder "God's peace and love flowing in and through him." Merton wrote in *New Seeds of Contemplation*:

It is above all in this silent and unconscious testimony to the love of God that the contemplative exercises his apostolate. For the saint preaches a sermon by the way he walks and the way he stands and the way he sits down and the way he picks things up and holds them in his hand. They do not have to reflect on the details of their own actions. Less and less conscious of themselves, they finally cease to be aware of themselves doing things, and gradually God begins to do all that they do, in them and for them, at least in the sense that the habit of His love has become second nature to them and informs all that they do with His likeness. [103]

5. <u>Paradise and Social Reformation</u>

Does the Paradise Man fight for social justice? Of course he does. Merton cites a great representative for "social reformation" among the ranks of Paradise People. That representative was Mohandas Karamchand Gandhi. Gandhi, although an authentic Hindu, lived and acted also in the likeness of the Paradise Man we are getting to know in this book.

Just as a Paradise Man is in unity with Christ in all His members, Gandhi was united with God in all the sufferings of India and became, not only for India, but also for the whole world, the voice of the truth and love and unity of the whole of humankind. Merton writes of Gandhi:

Gandhi realized that the people of India were awakening in him. The masses who had been totally silent for thousands of years had now found a voice in him. It was not "Indian thought" or "Indian spirituality" that was stirring in him, but India herself. It was the spiritual consciousness of a people that awakened in the spirit of one person. But the message of the Indian spirit, of Indian wisdom,

was not for India alone. It was for the entire world. Hence Gandhi's message was valid for India and for himself, in so far as it represented the awakening of a new world. [104]

Not only for the unity of humanity, Gandhi spoke also for unity with God. If this is not only the voice of truth of the whole humankind, but also the voice of God Himself, who can stop the Mighty Word? He revealed an astounding truth for all politicians and for anyone who is concerned with social justice: that **"the public realm was not secular, it was sacred."** According to Merton:

Gandhi's public life was one of maximum exposure, and he kept it so. For him, the public realm was not secular, it was sacred. To be involved in it was then to be involved in the sacred dharma of the Indian people. Surrender to the demands of the dharma, to the sacred needs of the Harijan (outcasts, untouchables) and of all India, was purely and simply surrender to God and His will,

manifested in the midst of the people.
105

Politics, then, to Gandhi was the act of **"worship."** Meanwhile in the Church there has been a lot of discussion about its proper outreach to the helpless, e.g., Should the Church spend more time being involved in concrete social justice than in doing liturgy? As Jesus had done in making His legal punishment—which was His death on the cross— an act of worship, a sacrifice, so Gandhi made a wonderful synthesis for the above discussion in making both **"political acts"** and **"liturgical acts"** one.[106]

The message Gandhi offered to the world was Satyagraha (the power of truth). This truth could be understood as a logical truth which convinces people by the clarity of its reasoning, and it could also be understood as **"the Truth"** Who is God and Whose Power is **"Unlimited."**

The message of Gandhi taught that all humanity is one, that **"violence was wrong in indicating my brothers to be my enemies,"** that if I killed my brothers, I killed, thus, myself. The message also taught that I cannot remain silent and see my brothers doing wrong to each other. The religious duty of a follower of Satyagraha is to confront the **"untruths," to "unmask" all injustice "even if one has to suffer and die."**[107]

How did Gandhi witness the truth of unity? He did so by the "non-violence" approach. Gandhi witnessed to the truth of the unity of mankind and the love they should have for one another. His witness of endurance at any cost with suffering through "non-violence" showed to his persecutors a message that **"no matter what wrong you could do me, you will never be able to change your status of being my brothers. You will never become my enemies."**

Such witness can only be given by someone who has a real "love," and the more he loves the more powerful his witness becomes. That was why Gandhi considered **"Satyagraha"** not as a political tactic or a means to achieve unity and freedom, but as **"the fruit of inner unity and inner freedom already achieved."**[108]

Gandhi's way, as expressed above, was typical of a Paradise Man in doing social reformation. His belief in unity, in God, in love, in truth, and his approach that was action and witness, revealed his state of paradise life. He smiled and felt happy in the midst of struggle and conflict, of torture and fasting. His witnessing was incredible. He even told his secret of paradise: **"The surrender to God."** The story goes as follows:

When friends tried to dissuade Gandhi from fasting for people (and Gandhi's fasts were completely public, political acts in the highest sense of the word) he replied:

> **God's voice has been increasingly audible as years have rolled by. He has never forsaken me even in my darkest hour. He has saved me often against myself and left me not a vestige of independence. The greater the surrender to Him, the greater has been my joy.** [109]

6. <u>Paradise in Ordinary Lifestyles</u>

In the first parts of this book, it seemed that the focus was given to mystics (in union with God), artists and poets and writers (in union with the poetic and aesthetic world), and heroes and great saints (in union with others) because they had great virtues and have done great actions in reforming the world. Does paradise have room also for the blind, the deaf, the handicapped, the unintelligent, the ugly, the unlearned, the poor? Fortunately, paradise is first of all the reward to all those who cannot do great things, who have nothing except God, as Jesus promised them:

Happy are those who know they are spiritually poor; the Kingdom of Heaven belongs to them!

Happy are those who mourn; God will comfort them!

Happy are those who are humble; they will receive what God has promised!

Happy are those whose greatest desire is to do what God requires; God will satisfy them fully!

Happy are those who are merciful to others; God will be merciful to them!

Happy are the pure of heart; they will see God!

Happy are those who work for peace; God will call them His children!

Happy are those who are persecuted because they do what God requires; The Kingdom of Heaven belongs to them!

Happy are you when people insult you and persecute you and tell all kinds of evil lies against you because

**you are my followers. Be happy and
glad for a great reward is kept for you
in heaven! (Matthew 10:3-12)**

Saint Benedict, by his Rule brought the emphasis
of monastic disciplines away from the "heroic"
tendency or extraordinary performance of the
monks of earlier centuries, and brought it back
to the ordinary tasks in daily life. Holiness was
relocated from outer works to the quality of inner
love. Saint Benedict, thus, understood the intention
of Christ who chose His twelve apostles not from the
well-known ascetics, but from the ordinary folks:
"workmen, fishermen and publicans." [110]

Thomas Merton observes that, among those who
followed religious vocations, the ones who did not
try to do the exceptional, but tried to keep faithfully
their daily duty of the common rule, were those who
stayed. They were generally "the normal, good-
humored, patient, obedient ones." [111]

These hidden paradise people are also found to
be the "sages" of Tao. Merton described the Oriental
saints in many images:

**The "sage," or the man who has
discovered the secret of the Tao, has
not acquired any special esoteric**

knowledge that sets him apart from others and makes him smarter than they are. On the contrary, he is from a certain point of view more stupid and exteriorly less remarkable. He is "dim and obscure." While everyone else exults over success as over a sacrificial ox, he alone is silent, "like a babe who has not yet smiled." Though he has in fact "returned to the root," the Tao, he appears to be the "only one who has no home to return to." He is very much like the one who has nowhere to lay his head, even though the foxes may have holes and the birds of the air their nests. He who has found the Tao has no local habitation and no name on the earth. He is "blank like the ocean, aimless as the wafting gale." Again, we remember the Gospels: "The wind blows where it pleases . . . even so is every man who is born of the Spirit." (John 3:8)[112]

The ordinary Paradise Man understands best what life is. He rejoices in the richness of life which is not necessarily the limited result of his own achievement, but which is the wholeness of life already achieved by God's hand. That is why at the end of the sixth day of creation, God looked upon His work of creating all things in the universe including humankind. He beheld and evaluated it: It was very good.

Thomas Merton wrote in *The Silent Life* about the peace and value of simple works of humble monks in monasteries because of God's presence filling all those activities, making them precious:

> **The victory of monastic humility is the full acceptance of God's hidden action in the weakness and ordinariness and unsatisfactoriness of our own everyday lives. It is the acceptance of our own incompleteness, in order that He may make us complete in His own way. It is joy in our emptiness, which can only be filled by Him. It is peace in our own unfruitfulness which He Himself makes immensely fruitful without our being able to understand how it is done.**[113]

Paradise appears, therefore, in very little things: the joys of simple people, the wonder in the eyes of children who were said to be owners of the Kingdom of God. (Mt. 18 3-4) Paradise is in little things:

Little Things

It's just the little homely things
The unobtrusive, friendly things,
The "won't-you-let-me-help-you" things
That makes our pathway light--
And it's just the jolly, joking things,
The "never-mind-the-trouble" things
The "laugh-with-me, it's funny" things
That makes the world seem bright.

Author Unknown

According to Thomas Merton, you need not be a bishop, a priest, a monk, a nun, a religious or a hermit; you may be a lay person, a normal churchgoer very busy with your daily duties, but you certainly could also be a Paradise Man.

It would be very happy for a pastor if there would come a Sunday when he could look around his church filled up with those simple and regular parishioners who were all self-forgetting and who could not hide the brilliant light of God's presence in their hearts and on their faces. These people would make his parish a paradise, and when they went back home, they would enjoy their own paradise families. At each house people would find a paradise dad, a paradise mom and a bunch of paradise boys and girls. This is not just a beautiful dream of a pastor, rather it is becoming a reality because the will of God the Father requires that everything be recapitulated by God the Son, back into the good order of a New Heaven and a New Earth. (Eph 1.22; Rev 21, 1-4)

7. <u>Christ: The Second Adam</u>

In paradise the Paradise Man is in union with all human beings, but he enjoys the most in keeping relationship with Jesus Christ. That is the well known villager of Nazareth, who is a lovely person with an extraordinarily charming character, a profound religious master, the most influent speaker of the world, a holy personality above all saints. If one looks for a true good friend, come to Him; if one wants to find a good adviser to solve troubles, come to Him; if one wants a holy person to pray for needs, come to Him; if you are fearful and want somebody to protect you, come to Him. Though embracing the finest qualities, He is easy to approach because He is extremely simple and humble, gentle and meek. Therefore even children, sinners and outcast people like to meet and talk to Him. All those who are saints just try to imitate Him. Let us inquire for which significant reasons the Paradise Man gets interested in this very special and mysterious man named Jesus Christ.

a) <u>First, Christ bridged the gap between God and us</u>

God is the Creator and Origin of everything including Paradise. Therefore, in search of Paradise humans must look for God. However, God in His transcendent nature is inaccessible to humans. Therefore, there is always an infinite gap between God and us. How can we pass this gap? How can we build a ladder long enough for us to climb from earth to heaven? It is an impossible thing though we build for a thousand years, though for billion years. Human beings with their limitedness must stay forever on this side of the gap, longing for God on the other side. Thankfully, Christ has come as our Hero. The first favor He did for us, humankind, was to fill that infinite gap between God and us. It is through Him, with Him and in Him that humans are connected with God and become Paradise people. Therefore the Paradise man never forgets this first favor which Christ did for him. Christ was able to do this incredible task of bridging the infinite gap because He is also God, the Divine Son of Almighty God. He came down to earth in the form of a human being and became the God-Man. From then on human beings could come back to Paradise and live in union with God again. Thomas Merton expressed this point in his book *New Seeds of Contemplation:*

> **For in Christ God is made Man. In him God and Man are no longer separate, remote from one another, but inseparably one, unconfused and yet indivisible. Hence in Christ everything that is divine and supernatural becomes accessible on the human level to every man born of woman, to every son of Adam.** [114]

b) <u>Second, Christ is the Light of the world.</u>

Christ came to the earth. On each anniversary of the day He came, Christmas, all churches celebrate the central theme: "The Light of the world". In echoing this theme, all Christians, religious and lay, sing the canticle *"Benedictus"* of Zechariah in their morning prayer throughout the year:

> **Because of the tender mercy of our God by which the daybreak from on high will visit us to shine on those who sit in darkness and death's shadow, to guide our feet into the path of peace."** (Luke 1:78-79)

Holy Scripture tells of three wise kings representing all nations, who kept following the light of the guiding star to find Him and paid their homage and offered Him their gifts. (Matthew 2:1-12)

He gave light in human manner by teaching the words of truth, which are the words of God, His Father:

> **"In times past, God spoke in partial and various ways to our ancestors through the prophets; in these last days, he spoke to us through a son, whom he made heir of all things and through whom he created the universe."** (Hebrews 1: 1-2)

Jesus Christ, as the Incarnated God, spent three years in teaching people the way to perfection. Thomas Merton wrote about this point in *Life and Holiness*:

> **Perfection is not a moral embellishment which we acquire outside of Christ, in order to qualify for union with him. . . . In order that we may attain to Christian perfection, Jesus has left us his teachings, the Sacraments of the Church, and all the counsels by which he shows us the way to live more perfectly in him and for him.** [115]

In His teaching He shakes the hearts and minds of people. The truths he taught are challenging guidance. They are worth being called the teachings of Heaven. Following are a few citations of His precious teachings from the *Gospel according to Matthew:*

> **"You have heard that it was said, 'An eye for an eye and a tooth for a tooth.' But I say to you, offer no resistance to one who is evil. When**

someone strikes you on [your] right cheek, turn the other one to him as well. If anyone wants to go to law with you over your tunic, hand him your cloak as well. Should anyone press you into service for one mile, go with him for two miles. Give to the one who asks of you, and do not turn your back on one who wants to borrow."

"You have heard that it was said, 'You shall love your neighbor and hate your enemy.' But I say to you, love your enemies, and pray for those who persecute you, that you may be children of your heavenly Father, for he makes his sun rise on the bad and the good, and causes rain to fall on the just and the unjust. For if you love those who love you, what recompense will you have? Do not the tax collectors do the same? And if you greet your brothers only, what is unusual about that? Do not the pagans do the same? So be perfect, just as your heavenly Father is perfect. (Matthew 5: 38-48)

In a challenging world where people daily fight against one another as wolves for their own egos, people are very shocked by the above merciful teachings of Jesus Christ. But He sternly continued preaching about His central theme on Charity. When Simon Peter the apostle asked him how many times had he to forgive others, whether it should be seven times, Jesus answered, **"I say to you, not seven times but seventy-seven times."** (Mt. 18: 21-22)

Jesus Christ had superb talent in teaching by using parables which make messages easy to understand and attractive to listen to, and the most beautiful parable is that of the Prodigal Son. This story has made numberless people in all ages shed tears because it was similar to the story of their own lives. The deep love of an earthly father demonstrates excellently the unlimited merciful love of God, the Heavenly Father. (Luke 15:11-32)

Our human life is full of anxiety and fear, but with beautiful words He taught us not to worry too much about life:

> **"Therefore I tell you, do not worry about your life, what you will eat [or drink], or about your body, what you will wear. Is not life more than food and**

the body more than clothing? Look at the birds in the sky; they do not sow or reap, they gather nothing into barns, yet your heavenly Father feeds them. Are not you more important than they? Can any of you by worrying add a single moment to your life-span? Why are you anxious about clothes? Learn from the way the wild flowers grow. They do not work or spin. But I tell you that not even Solomon in all his splendor was clothed like one of them. If God so clothes the grass of the field, which grows today and is thrown into the oven tomorrow, will he not much more provide for you, O you of little faith? (Mt 6: 25-30)

True religion is not a noisy outward show, but an internal and secret relationship with God:

"When you pray, go to your inner room, close the door, and pray to your Father in secret. And your Father who sees in secret will repay you." (Mt 6:6) **"When you fast, anoint your head and wash your face that your fasting may**

not be seen by men but by your Father who is in secret; and your Father who sees in secret will reward you." (Mt 6:17-18)

Sanctity is realized by beginning with a thought from inside, not waiting for an outside action. Jesus taught:

"You have heard that it was said, You shall not commit adultery. But I say to you, everyone who looks at a woman with lust has already committed adultery with her in his heart (Mat 5:27-28)

"There is nothing outside a man which by going into him can defile him; but the things which come out of a man are what defile him. . . From within people, from their hearts, come evil thoughts, unchastity, theft, murder, adultery, greed, malice, deceit, licentiousness, envy, blasphemy, arrogance, folly. All these evils come from within and they defile." (Mk 7:15, 21-23)

However, the most important and central lesson that He taught is fraternal love:

This is my commandment, that you love one another as I have loved you. Greater love has no man than this that a man lay down his life for his friends. (John 15: 12-14)

c) <u>Third, Christ sacrified and died to save the human world.</u>

The third favor which humankind owes to Christ is His immense love given to us, even unto death. He did not only teach, but he acted as an example about the great love "daring to lay his life for his friends". He sacrificed for us in accepting a painful death on the cross to erase all sins of humanity. The object of His redemption is all the sins of humankind, from the first sin of the first human being who is Adam unto the last sin of the last human being at the end of the world. And His sacrifice done only one time is enough. [Hebrews 7, 27] Because by nature He is God, His sacrifice brought an infinite merit. Therefore His death brought total freedom back to all human beings.

Saint Paul, expressed his extreme admiration for Christ and especially for His Name "Jesus" which God the Father chose for His own Son, in the letter to the community of Philippians:

Who, though he was in the form of God, did not regard equality with God something to be grasped. Rather, he emptied himself, taking the form of a slave, coming in human likeness; and found human in appearance, he humbled himself, becoming obedient to death, even death on a cross. Because of this, God greatly exalted him and bestowed on him the name that is above every name, that at the name of Jesus every knee should bend, of those in heaven and on earth and under the earth, and every tongue confess that Jesus Christ is Lord, to the glory of God the Father.(Philippians 2:6-11)

Saint Thomas Aquinas, an eminent doctor of the Church, in one of the popular prayers written by him, *Adoro te devote* (I devoutly adore you), said that Christ by His Divine Nature needed only just one drop of blood to purify the whole world. Following is a stanza of that prayer:

O loving Pelican! O Jesus Lord!
Unclean I am, but cleanse me in thy
Blood!
Of which a single drop, for sinners
spilt
Can purge the entire world from
all its guilt.

Actually, did Christ pour only one drop to save humankind? No, He poured all the blood He had for us. There were maybe a million drops. Thus He merited forgiving grace a million times more than necessary. It shows what immense love He has for each person in humankind. The holes in His hands and feet which He showed to the apostle Thomas, and in the side, and the wounds made by thorns on His head, and the cuts made by rods all over His body, as saints said, held the deep secret of His immense divine mercy. How should each human respond to His ocean of love?!

d) <u>Fourth, Christ recovered paradise for humankind</u>

The fourth grand gift we owe to Christ is the recovery of Paradise. The estate which had been once our inheritance but lost by our First Ancestor Adam, was recovered by Christ, our Second Adam, through the sacrifice of His life. Merton wrote in *Bread in the Wilderness*:

> **The Psalms (Gradual Psalms) teach us the way back to paradise. Christ died that we might recover all that Adam lost in Eden and more besides.** [116]

Thomas Merton recalled the teaching of Desert Fathers in *The Silent Life*:

> **The Desert Fathers knew this well. One of them, Abbot Isaias, expounds the traditional doctrine of the Fathers: that man, made in the image of God, was made for perfect union with Him. Having lost the capacity for union by Adam's sin, he had recovered it in Christ. Through Christ man returns**

to the original perfection intended for human nature by God. The Christian life is therefore a return to "paradise", a partial restoration of the joy and peace of Adam's contemplative life in Eden. In saving man, the passion of Christ has also healed his body and all his faculties, and indeed the sanctifying power of the Cross has poured itself upon the whole world, and man is once again able to find God in himself and in everything else.[117]

The Christian life is the return to "paradise". When one lives truly and fully a Christian life, he begins walking in Paradise. Paradise was regained through Christ. The flaming sword and the Cherubim were also taken away. Every single child of the human race is entitled to return. We need only say farewell to the world of exile established by the ego to return to the innocent original world of Adam just as before the fall.

However, the Paradise which Christ regained for humankind has higher value than the Paradise lost by the sin of Adam, in *The New Man* Merton contrasts our natural heritage from Adam with our greater heritage from Christ.

> **". . . Saint Paul prescinds from that in this text (I Corinthians 15:45) in which he is considering Adam's actual paternity – by which only natural life is transmitted to us. But Christ gives us more than a natural life. He is the source and principle of a life that is "heavenly" that is to say divine." [118]**

The regained Paradise is not the repetition of the original Paradise, but a totally new spiritual creation:

> **Just as Adam is the one chosen by God to preside over the first creation, Christ is sent by Him to institute and govern an entirely new spiritual Creation. For with the death and resurrection of Christ we are in a new world, a new age. The fullness of time has come. The history of the world has achieved an entirely new orientation. We are living in the Messianic Kingdom. [119]**

e) **Fifth, Christ is the exemplary and sustaining cause of all human beings**

We owe a profound debt to Christ not only for His work of redemption and the recovery of paradise, but for His presence even at the first moment of our creation Christ was present there as our exemplary cause and afterwards as sustaining cause for our existence as well as for all other creatures including Adam, the first person and progenitor of human race. In *The New Man* Thomas Merton recalled the teaching of Apostle Saint Paul:

> **The cosmic mediation of Christ is brought out clearly in St. Paul's Captivity Epistles, especially in the one to the Colossians. Here he says: "He is the image of the invisible God, the firstborn of all creation. For in him were created all things in heaven and on earth, the visible and the invisible, whether thrones or dominions or principalities or powers; all things were created through him and for him. He is before all things, and in him all things hold together."** (Colossians 1:15-17)

And Thomas Merton commented:

In reading words like these, one is astounded that they receive so little attention from Christians today. It is the Man-God, the Redeemer, Who is the "firstborn of every creature" and who is consequently "born" before Adam. Christ comes before Adam not only because He is more perfect, has more exalted dignity, a greater power, but also because in Him Adam is created, like everything else in Heaven and on earth. All creatures, spiritual and material are created in, through and by Christ, the Word of God. And He is "before all creatures" – their beginning, their source as well as the end. Furthermore, it is He Who sustains them in being. In Him they "hold together." Without Him they would fall apart. [120]

With vigorous expression, an anonymous writer added more on the above great truths of Christ as exemplary cause of creation:

St. Thomas Aquinas held the following principle: *that which is most perfect is always the exemplar of that which is less perfect* **(cf.** *Summa Theologiae***, III, 56, 1ad3). Christ, the "image of the invisible God" (Col 1:15, 2Cor 4:4), the perfect micro-cosmos, is the exemplar cause of all creation (as well as its re-creation). In the prologue of St. John's Gospel we hear: "All things came to be through him, and without him nothing came to be. . . He was in the world, and the world came to be through him," (Jn. 1:3, 10; cf. Heb 1:2). Christ, therefore, is the universal prototype, foundation and blueprint of all creation . . ."** [121]

The same writer recalled the teaching of Saint Lawrence Brindisi, Doctor of the Church, about the leading and creating role of Christ, The Second Adam, in the order of all creation and His superior position in comparing with First Adam:

Using the writings of many fathers like Jerome, Hilary, Cyril and Theodoret, St. Lawrence of Brindisi

explains that man is made in the image of Christ, Who is both God and man, teaching: "Christ was first predetermined in the Divine Mind, as the Psalm says, 'In the head of the book it is written of me,' because He is 'the firstborn of every creature.' However, the Christ was determined, not according to divine nature, but human nature, because the Divine Mind before everything else conceived the form that the Word-to-be-Incarnate would receive. God, then, created the first man [Adam] in the image and likeness of that form. Accordingly, Scripture says that 'in the image of God,' namely of the Incarnation, i.e., Christ, Who is God, 'He created him' (Gen. 1:27) (St. Lawrence of Brindisi on *Creation and the Fall, Gen 1:27).* In Michelangelo's now famous scene of Adam's creation on the ceiling of the Sistine Chapel, God the Father reaches out to give Adam life with His right finger while His left is pointing and resting on the Christ Child with

His Blessed Mother. God is saying, "Adam, We are creating you in the image of the Christ... and we are creating for the Christ." [122]

Paradise people take care to reflect on the important favors accomplished for us by the most special Paradise Man, Jesus Christ, Who filled the infinite gap between God and men; Who was light shining in the blind world and led people into the way of truth and wisdom; Who died horribly for every human's sins and opened again the gate of Paradise; Who was the Word of Almighty God, so that through Him all creatures got their exemplary image; and Who is still sustaining the existence of each creature because without His support everything would fall back into nothingness; and paradise people imitating the apostle Thomas, bow before the God-Man. They call His sweet Name with joyful and loving hearts in the most admiring and cheerful voices: "My Lord, My God!"

Meditating on the profound favors the Son of God did for us and on the immense love He has, especially on the sight of Him being hung on the cross and dying on the hill top of Calvary, many of humankind have responded in action. Thousands of brave hearts voluntarily shed their blood, bearing all kinds of tortures, and died for His Name in their heroic martyrdom; thousands of virgins voluntarily make their vows of virginity for Him, their Love and their God; thousands of monks and nuns willingly spend their lives in silence and solitude, faithfully celebrating their daily prayer with Him; thousands and thousands of men and women in religious organizations following His teaching dedicate their lives in active charity, to reach out and heal all kinds of spiritual and physical wounds in humankind; and millions of lay people contribute to create a better world in the His Name; and yearly on Christmas, all of them, over two billion Christians, with their families and friends, fill their churches on earth to celebrate the birthday of Him, the Christ, the Second Adam, the Greatest Paradise Man and Savior of all humankind.

CONCLUSION

CONCLUSION

We have just read through three chapters about the spiritual life of Paradise Man, his interior life in union with God, with Creation and with Human World. As the introduction stated, the purpose of this work is to help readers who are churchgoers and the author himself find more inspiration for their spiritual journey. If you are a churchgoer and after slowly reading thoroughly the above chapters and you like it, or you agree with Thomas Merton and other contributors on some points; if you really like the way of the Paradise Man in praying, his way of treating the poor and the suffering people in the world, his way of cherishing everything in nature and revering their sacredness and wonder; if you feel that the way of the Paradise Man might contribute a little to your way of life; then this book is successful and has reached its goal. However, if you say "I want to become a Paradise Man myself", then, hurray! hurray! This work hits its jackpot! Certainly you can do it and certainly you are eligible for it because Paradise belongs to everyone on earth. In fact you are already a Paradise Man all along since your birth, but you now know about it. We all are Paradise People since two thousand years ago when the Son of God died for us on the top of the hill to regain Paradise for us. We all are like those who are sleeping and we just need an act of awakening which Meister Eckhart calls a "breakthough".

The original paradise and the present paradise are both different and similar. The original human society was only a small family with two people, Adam and Eve, a small world with a lot of intimacy, but the human society today is a huge paradise with over 7.3 billion people living in 195 countries. The two paradises are therefore quite different. The human world today is much livelier in communication, complex in cultural varieties, joyful in sport, music and arts, wise in communal organization and regulation. The increase in number makes every aspect of life become important and great. They escalate according to the size of the group: a village, a region, a nation and global world. People today are very proud of their civilization and technology. However, in depth the two human worlds are not different. There are still the same principles of life in one person as well as in 7.3 billion people. There is the same basic effort to find out how to live happily. The same dignity in having freedom but nonetheless the great challenge in how to use it rightly. Especially, the only condition to live in paradise is still purity of heart. It is still the happy paradise of living in union with God, with the World and with the Humankind.

Paradise seems to be unreal to many, but in truth, Paradise is as real as our daily life. It is as real as birds in the forest, clouds drifting in the sky and sweat running down the faces of farmers. Paradise is as real as children running, singing and playing in the street, as a butterfly flying on flowers, as a mother joyfully smiling with her new-born child, as a beautiful smile on a maiden's face, as a fisherman sitting in his boat and listening to the sound of the waves, a cool breeze passing through leaves making murmuring sound and vibrating the surface of a lake. Thomas Merton wrote in his work *Conjectures by a Guilty Bystander*:

"Paradise is all around us and we do not understand. It is wide open. The sword is taken away, but we do

not know it; we are off "one to his farm and another to his merchandise" [123]

A friend asked me why *The Paradise World* had to begin with union with God. He meant: why didn't we alone create a paradise so that we alone could stay there and freely enjoy it, a completely human paradise without God? I find this is an interesting and important question. There have been many people who think and dream that way. My answer is that we look for God in our Paradise for three reasons: politeness, gratitude and necessity.

For politeness and gratitude: this is for churchgoers who believe in God. Watching the great works which God did in creating this beautiful earth and creation including the immense universe, they respect and revere Him. Therefore when they are thinking about stepping into the Paradise World, the first thought which comes to their mind is that "I am entering the estate of God." The should-be gesture of every churchgoer is first visiting God, the Owner of the Paradise, to greet Him, to recognize His ownership, express admiration and to thank Him for all convenient and delightful wonders of God which make life and the world so enjoyable. We are like a group of playing children. The joyful and innocent game led them to the front of a beautiful house which they haven't seen. They open the door and enter. It is beautiful inside. All ornaments and interior decorations are precious objects. At their surprise when they enter the dining room, delicious food is already cooked and put on table. Some kids go right in, sit down and eat without thinking because they are all hungry, but a well trained boy says: "Wait! Who prepared these foods for us? Let's go to find the host and hostess to greet and thank them first before eating." Another boy says: "But we are hungry, we cannot wait. Let's eat and thank later!" The wise boy says: "Thus, let's say together in a loud voice: 'Thank you, host, for the good food!' Then eat." So they stand and, together making a loud voice, say the grateful sentence to the host, and sit down and enjoy the food. The invisible host and hostess are content before the well-behaved kids. They go prepare dessert for them because they deserve their treat.

For necessity: this is for all those who have dreamt to find or create a human paradise but no one has ever succeeded. Being unsatisfied with the reality of life in which humans wrestle with sufferings of all kinds: poverty, injustice, violence, illiteracy, malnutrition, unemployment, depression, illness, age, etc, they want to escape from this sad reality and they dream of a happy place where everything is perfect, everyone is perfect. There were talented authors who wrote and suggested reformation from the top administration of a state. Confucius (551-479 BC) in China opened a school, teaching his pupils how to make a happy nation. In Greece, the philosopher Plato (428-348) offered his vision about a perfect political system in his work *The Republic*. Plutarch (A.D.46-120) gave an idealized description of Sparta in his work *Lives*. Saint Thomas More (1478-1535) wrote the most famous book **Utopia** first published in Latin as *De optimo reipublicae statu, deque nova insula Utopia* in 1516, and it was translated into English in 1551. Utopia is a Greek word which means "No Where", but the same Utopia sounding Greek word "Eutopia" means "The Good Place". Utopia is about an imaginary Portuguese voyager who has made three voyages to America, he has come across an island named Utopia in which the government is ideal, everyone is equal, prosperous, educated and wise. "Utopia" or "Utopian" became the common name for the literature which has the same dream to build an ideal human society. In the seventeenth century other noted utopian works were written: *New Atlantis* (1624) by Francis Bacon, *Civitas Solis* (1623) by Tommaso Campanella,

Oceana (1656) by James Harrington. In eighteenth and nineteenth century we have Mercier's *L'An 2440* (1742), James Burgh's *Account of the Cessares* (1764), Bulwer Lytton's *The Coming Race* (1871), Samuel Butler's *Erewhon* (1872), Edward Bellany's *Looking Backward* (1888), William Morris's *News from Nowhere* (1890). And the twentieth century on ward has H.G. Wells'*Anticipations* (1901), *A Modern Utopia* (1905), Louis Blanc's *The Organization of Work* which coined the slogan "To each according to his need, from each according to his abilities." (1839), B. F. Skinner's *Walden Two* (1948). Among negative utopias are Aldous Huxley's *Brave New World* (1932), George Orwell's *Animal Farm* (1945) and *Nineteen Eighty-Four* (1949), each of them suffering under a wicked ruler. Of course, only wicked rulers have ever dared to say his nation is a paradise or a perfect state.

It seems easier to try to form a human paradise in a smaller scale: just a small community in isolation from the society at large. There were many experiments as such in the United States in 19th and 20th centuries: Shakers' Villages (1830) in Maine, New Harmony (1825), Oneida Communities (1848) in New York, Brook Farm (1841) supported by prominent Trancendentalists such as Ralph Waldo Emerson and his friends, the most recent effort is

Republic of Minerva (1971) by millionaire Michael Oliver in South Pacific Ocean. These communities existed only for a very short time. Some lasted for a few decades, but all dissolved as dreams. However the dream of a human paradise still continues and maintains itself in the heart of man in all ages. It keeps being a fervent desire in the hearts of students in universities of all nations, in their schools of Law, of Politics, in Military Academies, in schools of Business Administration, of Management, of Social Science where the students learn lessons in history and the rules how to create a best society, how to make the most successful company. They all keep dreaming and striving to make the dream come true, but until today there is not any human paradise which endures.

The failure of every human paradise or utopia is summed up in two sentences by *Encyclopedia Britannica*:

> **Utopia, an ideal commonwealth whose inhabitants exist under perfect conditions. Hence "utopian" is used to denote a visionary reform, which fails to recognize defects in human nature.** [124]

Exactly, the defects in human nature were the main causes of failure in all human paradises and utopias. Often the life and development of a human utopia depends on the spirit and ability of the founder who has a lot of defects in his own nature, leaving the human utopia in the status of uncertainty. If the founder fails in physical health because of illness or old age, he would lose courage and cancel the utopian project. If he fails in finance he cannot maintain the ideal community and he must quit. If he fails in the stability of morality and commits any sin, the community which he gathers may lose their trust and respect in him and they would leave. Founders and their human paradises are easily destroyed by natural disasters: fire, hurricane, floods. Divisiveness, impatience, jealousy, dissatisfaction among his followers can also cause the dissolution of the community. Though keeping all the ideal conditions, the founder will endure the mortal nature of humanity which is the death, the shortness of life, the passing fate of humanity, like a flower that blooms gorgeously in the morning and hurriedly withers in the evening. After the founder disappears, the utopia which was brought forth by him also disappears. In short, because of the defects, the limitation, the shortness of human nature, no human and his created human paradise could remain in time. They all disappear leaving only the Paradise of God. Therefore, out of necessity, we humankind, believers or non-believers, need God to have a true Paradise, the only Paradise which exists until the end of time.

"Purity of heart" is the entrance to the Paradise of God, and the first requirement to become a Paradise Man. Therefore before closing the book, we need to pay attention to this important issue. The Desert Fathers spent a long time in desert, keeping isolation from the sinful world, in order to attain the purity of heart. Abbot Cassian said:

> **For the sake of purity of heart we seek solitude, fasting, vigils, labors, poor clothing, reading and all other monastic virtues. Through these practices we hope to be able to keep our heart untouched by the assaults of all the passions, and by these steps we hope to ascend to perfect love.** (Cassian, Conference 1, vii, Migne P.L. 49:489)

However, the thing which defiles the heart the most is the presence of one's ego which implies an "egocentric" tendency to put itself as the center of the world. Thomas Merton wrote in *The Silent Life*:

The "impure" heart of fallen man is not merely a heart subject to carnal passion. "Purity" and "impurity" in this context mean something more than chastity. The "impure" heart is a heart filled with fears, anxieties, conflicts, doubts, ambivalences, hesitations, self-contradictions, hatreds, jealousies, compulsive needs and passionate attachments. All these and a thousand other "impurities" darken the inner light of the soul but they are neither its chief impurity nor the cause of its impurities. The inner, basic, metaphysical, defilement of fallen man is his profound and illusory conviction that he is a god and that the universe is centered upon him. [125]

Religious men and women making vows of poverty denied themselves material possessions in order to become richer spiritually. However this effort if made without profound understanding, will cause their egos to grow even bigger. Their religious activities would not make them pure, but on the contrary, make them more impure because their egocentric souls get more self-exalted. Thomas Merton expressed this concern in his essay *"The Recovery of Paradise"* in his book *Selected Essays:*

> **The Desert Fathers realized that the most dangerous activities of the devil come into play against the monk only when he was morally perfect, that is, apparently "pure" and virtuous enough to be capable of spiritual pride. Then began the struggle with the last and subtlest of the attachments: The attachment to one's own spiritual excellence; the love of one's spiritualized, purified, and "empty" self, the narcissism of the perfect, of the pseudo-saint and of the false mystic. [126]**

The only escape from this dangerous situation is humility. According to Saint Teresa of Calcutta: **"Humility is walking in the Truth"** and as written in Scriptures **"Then you will know the truth, and the truth will set you free"** (John 8:32). What is the humble truth which one needs to know? The

Truth is that everything you have is from God, all the good works which you have done were done by the grace of God supporting you. Your own being is also a great gift created by God and given to you. That is the truth. Why do you dare to claim all credit for yourself? If one is fair one should admit the truth and praise God in everything. One will find God is all in all. One will be happy in union with God and be liberated from the pride of illusory ego. Humility will make one imitate Saint John the Baptist who said about Christ: **"He must increase; I must decrease"** (John 3:30). Thomas Merton wrote:

> **The only escape, as St. Anthony said, was humility. And the Desert Fathers' concept of humility corresponds very closely to the spiritual poverty Dr. Suzuki has just described for us. One must possess and retain absolutely nothing, not even a self in which he can receive angelic visitations, nor even a selflessness he can be proud of. True sanctity is not the work of man purifying himself; it is God Himself present in His own transcendent light, which to us is emptiness.** [127]

However, Paradise is not yet the ultimate end of our spiritual journey. Thomas Merton wrote about this last important point in the essay "The Recovery of Paradise" of his book *Selected Essays*:

> **One thing, and this is most important, remains to be said. Purity of heart is not the *ultimate end* of the monk's striving in the desert. It is only a step towards it. We have said above that Paradise is not yet Heaven. Paradise is not the final goal of the spiritual life. It is in fact, only a return to the true beginning. It is a "fresh start." The monk who has realized in himself purity of heart, and has been restored, in some measure, to the innocence lost by Adam, has still not ended his journey. He is only ready to begin.[128]**

The purity of heart is only the purifying step which liberates the Paradise Man from all the trouble of the illusory ego and gives back to him the innocent joy of a child in the Kingdom of God. It is just a fresh start of the greatest adventure in which God is the ultimate goal and the center of his life.

The journey toward the Almighty God in Heaven promises incredible findings and infinite happiness. The Paradise Man feels dizzy in observing the creation of God in a universe with more stars in space than grains of sand on earth. But this universe is like just a drop of water in comparing with its Creator, an immense ocean. However, the Paradise Man is not afraid because God is not a cold infinite space but He is a Living Spirit and a Loving Father.

To close this work, I would like to invite readers back to the divine ecology, to the "union life of paradise", to the "cosmic dance," in which God is the dancer and we are the dance. Thomas Merton wrote in *New Seeds of Contemplation:*

What in God might appear to us as "play" is perhaps what He Himself takes most seriously. At any rate, the Lord plays and diverts Himself in the garden of His creation, and if we could let go of our own obsession with what we think is the meaning of it all, we might be able to hear His call and follow Him in His mysterious, cosmic dance.

When we are alone on a starlit night; when by chance we see the migrating birds in Autumn descending on a grove of junipers to rest and eat; when we see children in a moment when they are really children; when we know love in our own hearts; or when, like the Japanese poet Basho, we hear an old frog land in a quiet pond with a solitary splash—at such times the awakening, the turning inside out of all values, the "newness," the emptiness and the purity of vision that makes themselves evident, provide a glimpse of the cosmic dance.[129]

That is all about the story of the Paradise Man!

APPENDICES

APPENDIX 1

GLOSSARY

1. **UTOPIA:** An imaginary place or state in which everything is perfect, originated by the book of Sir. Thomas More, which describes a place like this.
2. **TRANSCENDENT EXPERIENCE:** An out of the ordinary experience of the Ultimate or God; a direct encounter with the mysterious God of our Faith.
3. **EGO**: In psychology, a person's ordinary, conscious state; when referred to negatively the word suggests our self-centeredness
4. **ESSENCE**: The true nature of anything; the necessary qualities of any existing being. According to Aristotle, the human essence is to be a *rational animal.*
5. **IMMANENT GOD:** God present in His creation, the world, the human heart; the opposite of the **TRANSCENDENT QUALITY OF GOD,** who is ineffable and shrouded in mystery.
6. **EXISTENTIAL STRUCTURE OF THE SELF:** The actual existing nature of a person's consciousness.
7. **PSYCHOLOGICAL TRANSFORMATION:** A significant and radical change in one's Self-awareness, as in forgetfulness of the Self in God.
8. **PSYCHE;** The make-up of our individual human consciousness as it affects our lives.

9. **ACCIDENTAL PHENOMENON;** Non-essential qualities of any being or person, e.g., pride, spiritually or skin color, physically.

10. **ONTOLOGICAL TRANSFORMATION:** A change in our very nature as a result of God's activity in us.

11. **MYSTICAL BODY:** members of the Church bound together and to Christ through Baptism, with each person possessing some quality to contribute.

12. **ECSTASY:** An overpowering emotion; a sense of intense feeling in the experience of God; common to Mystics.

13. **MYSTIC:** A person with a deep experience of the mystery of the Transcendent God and/or a rich awareness of God's immanent qualities in nature or in ourselves.

14. **ASEITAS:** From Latin "a se" ("being for oneself") the "self-caused" and "uncaused" existence of God.

15. **BUDDHIST ZEN:** A Japanese form of Buddhism. Meditation, called "Za-zen" incorporating Yoga-like techniques, is employed for the purpose of encouraging the atmosphere of inner peace. In Zen Buddhism, Nirvana and Samsara are identical. One's usual life and the Tao are the same. The Buddha nature is in all men, so that all can become Buddha; and Buddha-mind is everywhere, so that anything can occasion its realization at any time. Enlightenment can hence be gained in the midst of ordinary living.

16. **CONTEMPLATION:** To look at with attention, to reflect, to meditate on.

17. **ADOLEZO PENO Y MUERO:** An expression in a poem of Saint John of The Cross, "I grow in pain and death."

18. **PRIMORDIAL EXPERIENCE:** occurring often in a state of ecstasy, carrying one to know the condition of original innocence.

19. **ESCHATOLOGY:** that branch of theology concerned with death and the last things; the end and renewal of the world when the eternal reign of Christ begins and all is fulfilled.

20. **FINITUDE:** Humankind's limited and imperfect nature.

21. **PASCHAL MYSTERY:** The events surrounding the death and Resurrection of Jesus the Christ, God and man.

22. **APOCALYPSE:** meaning the end of the world, is the last book of Bible, also called the Book of Revelation.

23. **PARADOX:** a person, thing or situation that has two opposite features and therefore seems strange. A statement seemingly absurd or self-contradictory, but really founded on truth.

24. **LABYRINTH:** a maze or a complicate series of paths, which it is difficult to find your way through.

25. **APOSTOLATE:** the participation by the *Mystical Body* in spreading Faith in Christ, the Church, its teachings and practices.

26. **INFUSED LOVE:** Love experienced by the free outpouring of the Holy Spirit to those who seek Union with God.

27. **TAO:** meaning "THE WAY" and the title of an important Chinese scripture by Lao-tse in the 6th century BCE.

28. **THEANDRIC WORK:** the union of the divine and human nature of Christ.

APPENDIX 2

PEOPLE

The information and texts of following entries are gathered from many sources among which Wikipedia is the most often consulted.

1. **ADAM and EVE:** The first man and woman, the progenitors of the human race.

2. **POPE FRANCIS:** His name is Jorge Mario Bergoglio. He was born December 17, 1936 in Flores, Buenos Aires, Argentina. He is current and the 266th Pope of the Roman Catholic Church. He chose Francis as his papal name in honor of Saint Francis of Assisi.

3. **ABRAHAM LINCOLN:** (1809-1865) born in Hodgenville, Kentucky; was the 16th President of the United States, serving from March 1861 until his assassination in April 1865. Lincoln led the United States through its Civil War—its bloodiest war and its greatest moral, constitutional, and political crisis. In doing so, he preserved the Union, abolished slavery, strengthened the federal government, and modernized the economy. Lincoln has been consistently ranked both by scholars and the public as one of the three greatest U.S. presidents.

4. **MARTIN LUTHER KING, JR:** Civil Rights leader Dr. Martin Luther King, Jr., born in Atlanta, Georgia, in 1929, never backed down in his stand against racism. He dedicated

his life to achieving equality and justice for all Americans of all colors. King believed that peaceful refusal to obey unjust law was the best way to bring about social change. He was considered one of the greatest speakers in American history. He received the Nobel Prize for Peace. King was assassinated by James Earl Ray on April 4, 1968 on the balcony of the Lorraine Motel. Americans honor the civil rights activist on the third Monday of January each year, Martin Luther King, Jr. Day.

5.   **DOROTHY DAY:** (1897 –1980) was an American journalist, social activist, and Catholic convert. She initially lived a bohemian lifestyle. Dorothy Day was born in Brooklyn, New York. She attended the University of Illinois at Urbana and became interested in radical social causes as a way to help workers and the poor. Dorothy had grown to admire the Catholic Church as the "Church of the poor." Her decision to have her daughter baptized and embrace the Catholic faith led to the end of her common law marriage and the loss of many of her radical friends. With Peter Maurin, a French immigrant and former Christian Brother, who had a vision for a society constructed of Gospel values. Together they founded the Catholic Worker newspaper which spawned a movement of houses of hospitality and farming communes that has been replicated throughout the United States and other countries. Her pilgrimage ended at Mary House in New York City on November 29, 1980, where she died among the poor.

6.   **DALAI LAMA:** His Holiness the 14th Dalai Lama, Tenzin Gyatso, describes himself as a simple Buddhist monk. He is the spiritual leader of Tibet. He was born on 6 July 1935, in a small hamlet located in northeastern Tibet. At 23, His Holiness was awarded the Geshe Lharampa degree, the highest-level degree, equivalent to a doctorate of Buddhist philosophy. In 1950 His Holiness forced to escape into exile. Since then he has been living in Dharamsala, northern India. In 1989 he was awarded the Nobel Peace Prize for his non-violent struggle for

the liberation of Tibet. His Holiness has travelled to more than 67 countries spanning 6 continents. He has also authored or co-authored more than 110 books.

7. **DESERT FATHERS:** (along with Desert Mothers) were early Christian hermits, ascetics, and monks who lived mainly in the Scetes desert of Egypt beginning around the third century AD. The most well known was Anthony the Great, who moved to the desert in 270–271 AD and became known as both the father and founder of desert monasticism. By the time Anthony died in 356 AD, thousands of monks and nuns had been drawn to living in the desert following Anthony's example — his biographer, Saint Athanasius of Alexandria, wrote that "the desert had become a city." The Desert Fathers had a major influence on the development of Christianity.

8. **DAISETZ SUZUKI:** *Suzuki Daisetsu Teitarō*; he rendered his name "Daisetz" in 1894; (18 October 1870 – 12 July 1966) was a Japanese author of books and essays on Buddhism, Zen and Shin that were instrumental in spreading interest in both Zen and Shin (and Far Eastern philosophy in general) to the West. Suzuki was also a prolific translator of Chinese, Japanese, and Sanskrit literature. Suzuki spent several lengthy stretches teaching or lecturing at Western universities, and devoted many years to a professorship at Otani University, a Japanese Buddhist school. He was nominated for the Nobel Peace Prize in 1963.

9. **MILTON:** John Milton was born in London on December 9, 1608, into a middle-class family. He was educated at St. Paul's School, then at Christ's College, Cambridge, where he began to write poetry in Latin, Italian, and English. He completed the blank-verse epic poem *Paradise Lost* in 1667, as well as its sequel *Paradise Regained* and the tragedy Samson Agonistes both in 1671. He died on November 8, 1674, in Buckinghamshire, England. *Paradise Lost*, which chronicles Satan's temptation of Adam and Eve and their expulsion from Eden, is widely regarded as his masterpiece and one of the

greatest epic poems in world literature. *Paradise Regained* expresses the effort of Satan in tempting Jesus in the desert but failed as written in Gospel of Saint Luke (4:1-13). Thus the Paradise according to Milton was lost by the disobedience of Adam, but it was regained by the obedience and faithfulness of Jesus Christ.

10. **E.M.W. TILLYARD:** Tillyard was born in Cambridge, where his father had served as mayor. He was educated at the Perse School and Jesus College. He was interest in the classics and archaeology, and in 1911 went to Athens to study at the British School of Archaeology. Tillyard was a Fellow in English (1926–1959) at Jesus College, later becoming Master (1945–1959). He is known mainly for his book *The Elizabethan World Picture* (1942), as background to Elizabethan literature, particularly Shakespeare, and for his works on John Milton.

11. **ST. TERESA OF AVILA:** (1515- 1582) born at Avila, Old Castile, Spain. She entered the Carmelite Convent of the Incarnation at Avila, which then counted 140 nuns. She came under the influence, first of the Dominicans, and afterwards of the Jesuits. Meanwhile God had begun to visit her with "intellectual visions and locutions". The whole city of Avila was troubled by the reports of the visions of this nun. The account of her spiritual life contained in the *"Life written by herself"*, in the *"Relations"*, and in the *"Interior Castle"*. After many troubles and much opposition, St. Teresa founded the convent of Discalced Carmelite Nuns of the Primitive Rule of St. Joseph at Avila (24 Aug., 1562). Four years later she received the visit of the General of the Carmelites, John-Baptist Rubeo (Rossi), who not only approved of what she had done but granted leave for the foundation of other convents of friars as well as nuns. Having made the acquaintance of Antonio de Heredia, prior of Medina, and St. John of the Cross, she established her reform among the friars. She passed away on 4 Oct., 1582. She was beatified in 1614, and canonized in 1622 by Pope Gregory XV.

12. **LUCIFER:** name of the devil and Satan, the chief angel who rebelled against God's rule in heaven. It is associated with the dragon in the book Revelation. He was also the tempter who persuaded Adam and Eve to offend God's commandment. Because of that sin of disobedience, the human first ancestors lost their paradise. (Genesis, chapter 3)

13. **SOLOMON:** God blessed Solomon with wisdom and understanding. His wisdom quickly became known worldwide and his wealth exceeded all the kings in the world. Solomon spoke 3,000 proverbs, wrote 1,005 songs, the book of Ecclesiastes and the Song of Solomon. He accumulated knowledge of trees, animals, birds, fish and more. Men came from all nations to hear the wisdom of Solomon. In his fourth year, King Solomon began building the TEMPLE OF THE LORD of the Lord according to the blueprints that God revealed to David. It was approximately 90 feet long by 30 feet wide, and three stories high. Almost 200,000 of his own people labored to transport materials to Jerusalem. The interior of the temple was decorated with detailed carvings and plated with over 20 tons of gold. It took seven years to construct. Although God had forbidden marriages between Israelites and people of other nations (Deuteronomy 7:1-4) in Solomon's latter years, he did all these things. He built places of worship for the gods of his foreign wives, and they turned his heart from the true God. He even participated in their rituals. This displeased God and He said to Solomon, *"Because you have done this, I will surely tear the kingdom away from you and give it to your servant. Nevertheless I will not do it in your days, for the sake of your father David. I will give one tribe to your son for the sake of My servant David, and for the sake of Jerusalem which I have chosen."* This was soon to be fulfilled with Jeroboam, and Solomon's son, Rehoboam. Solomon reigned 40 years until his death, ending the golden years of Israel.

14. **ST. BERNARD OF CLAIVAUX** (1090 –1153) the founding abbot of Clairvaux Abbey in Burgundy, France, was one of

the greatest spiritual masters of all times. He was born in Fontaines-les-Dijon in 1090 and entered the Abbey of Citeaux in 1112, bringing thirty of his relatives with him, including five of his brothers—his youngest brother and his widowed father followed later. After receiving a monastic formation from Saint Stephen Harding, he was sent in 1115 to begin a new monastery near Aube: Clairvaux, the Valley of Light. As a young abbot he published a series of sermons on the Annunciation. Bernard's spiritual writing as well as his extraordinary personal magnetism began to attract many to Clairvaux and the other Cistercian monasteries, leading to many new foundations. He personally saw to the establishment of sixty-five of three hundred Cistercian monasteries founded during his thirty-eight years as abbot. Bernard's dynamism soon reached far beyond monastic circle. He was sought as an advisor and mediator by the ruling powers of his age. Because of schisms which had arisen in the Church, he travelled all about Europe restoring peace and unity. He wrote many theological and spiritual works. His masterpiece, his Sermons on the Song of Songs, was begun in 1136 and was still in composition at the time of his death. He died in 1153 and was canonized by Pope Alexander III in 1174. Pope Pius VII declared him a Doctor of the Church in 1830.

15. **MOSES:** is a prophet in Abrahamic religions. According to the Hebrew Bible, he was a former Egyptian prince who later in life became a religious leader and lawgiver, to whom the authorship of the Torah is traditionally attributed. He is the most important prophet in Judaism. He is also an important prophet in Christianity, Islam, Bahá'ísm. After killing an Egyptian slavemaster because the slavemaster was smiting a Hebrew to death, Moses fled across the Red Sea to Midian, where he encountered the Angel of the Lord, speaking to him from within a burning bush on Mount Horeb which he regarded as the Mountain of God. God sent Moses back to Egypt to demand the release of the Israelites from slavery. After the Ten

Plagues, Moses led the Exodus of the Israelites out of Egypt and across the Red Sea, after which they based themselves at Mount Sinai, where Moses received the Ten Commandments. After 40 years of wandering in the desert, Moses died within sight of the Promised Land.

16.   **ETIENNE GILSON:** (1884 –1978) a French philosopher and historian of philosophy. A scholar of medieval philosophy, he originally specialized in the thought of Descartes, later in the teaching of Thomas Aquinas. He was graduated in Sorbonne University, France. He taught at the University of Lille, Strasbourg, Harvard, Toronto. In 1946 he was elected an "Immortal" (member) of the Académie Française. He influenced Thomas Merton in understanding of God as Aseitas and turned him into a convert to Catholic Church.

17.   **PIERRE TEILHARD DE CHARDIN:** (1881 –1955) was a French idealist philosopher and Jesuit priest who trained as a paleontologist and geologist and took part in the discovery of Peking Man. He conceived the idea of the Omega Point (a maximum level of complexity and consciousness towards which he believed the universe was evolving) and developed Vladimir Vernadsky's concept of noosphere. During his lifetime, many of Teilhard's writings were censored by the Catholic Church because of his views on original sin. Recently Teilhard has been praised by Pope Benedict XVI and other eminent Catholic figures. The response to his writings by evolutionary biologists has been, with some exceptions, decidedly negative.

18.   **MEISTER ECKHART**: (1260-1328) with full name Eckhart Von Hochhiem, O.P., was a German theologian, philosopher and mystic, came in prominence during the Avignon papacy. He had celebrated disciples: John Tauler, Henry Suso, Nicholas of Cusa, Eckhart Tolle and Gustav Landauer. Since 19th century he has received a renewed attention and interest by scholars within the Medieval Scholastic and Philosophical tradition.

19. **HENRI LE SAUX:** (Swami Abhishiktananda) (1910-1973) born in Brittany, France. In 1929 he entered the Benedictine Monastery of St. Anne de Kergonan. Fr. Le Saux was given permission by his abbot to go to India in 1948. A profoundly decisive event in his life was his meeting with Sri Ramana Maharshi. Swami Abhishiktananda spent several weeks and months in the caves of Arunachala between 1950 and 1955 in deep meditation. He also made several pilgrimages to the Himalayas. In 1973 Abhishiktananda suffered a heart attack on the road in Rishikesh, which he survived for only six months. He described this experience as a great spiritual awakening. Fr. Le Saux had come to experience Christ within the context of Advaita, the Vedanta of non-duality. Henri Le Saux (Swami Abhishiktananda) was the author of many books including *Saccidananda: A Christian Experience of Advaita*, *The Secret of Arunachala*, and *The Further Shore*. A collection of several of his essays appeared posthumously as *The Eyes of Light*.

20. **SAINT PAUL, Apostle** (c. 5 – c. 67), also known by his native name **Saul of Tarsus**, was an apostle (though not one of the Twelve Apostles) who taught the gospel of the Christ to the 1st-century world. He is generally considered one of the most important figures of the Apostolic Age. In the mid-30s to the mid-50s AD, he founded several churches in Asia Minor and Europe. Paul took advantage of his status as both a Jew and a Roman citizen to minister to both Jewish and Roman audiences. According to writings in the New Testament, Paul was dedicated to the persecution of the early disciples of Jesus in the area of Jerusalem. In the narrative of the book of Acts of the Apostles, Paul was traveling on the road from Jerusalem to Damascus on a mission to "bring them which were there bound unto Jerusalem" when the Resurrected Jesus appeared to him in a great light. He was struck blind, but after three days, under the order of Jesus his sight was restored by Ananias of Damascus, and Paul began to preach that Jesus of Nazareth is the Jewish Messiah and the Son of God. Approximately

half of the book of Acts deals with Paul's life and works. Fourteen of the twenty-seven books in the New Testament have traditionally been attributed to Paul. Today, Paul's epistles continue to be vital roots of the theology, worship, and pastoral life in the Catholic and Protestant traditions of the West, and the Orthodox traditions of the East. Eusebius of Caesarea in his *Church History* (320 AD) testifies that Paul was beheaded in Rome and Peter crucified.

21. **WILLIAM BLAKE:** (1757 – 1827) was an English poet, painter, and printmaker. Largely unrecognized during his lifetime, Blake is now considered a seminal figure in the history of the poetry and visual arts of the Romantic Age. His prophetic works have been said to form "what is in proportion to its merits the least read body of poetry in the English language." His visual artistry led one contemporary art critic to proclaim him "far and away the greatest artist Britain has ever produced". In 2002, Blake was placed at number 38 in the BBC's poll of the 100 Greatest Britons. Although Blake was considered mad by contemporaries for his idiosyncratic views, he is held in high regard by later critics for his expressiveness and creativity, and for the philosophical and mystical undercurrents within his work.

22. **ANTHONY IN THE DESERT:** (251-356) called the Patriarch of monks, born in Egypt, when his parents died at the age of 18, he distributed his property to the poor and beginning a life of penance he retired in the solitude of the desert. He attracted disciples and was the first abbot to form a stable rule for his community of monks. He supported believers during the persecution of Diocletian and assisted Saint Athanasius against the Arians.

23. **TOLTECS:** a member of an ancient group of Nahuatl Indians who lived in Mexico before the Aztecs: their culture shows Mayan influence.

24. **AZTECS:** a people with an advanced civilization still living in Mexico at the time of the Spanish invasion under Cortes in 1519.

25. **CARL SAGAN:** (1934 - 1996) was an American astronomer. Carl Sagan was born in Brooklyn, New York City, attended the University of Chicago earning two degrees in physics. He followed with a doctorate in Astronomy in 1960 and taught at Harvard University until 1968, when he moved to Cornell University. He tried to make science popular. He thought about what life from other planets would be like. He said that people should look for life on other planets. He is world famous for his popular science books and the television series *Cosmos*, which he co-wrote and presented. He wrote *Pale Blue Dot: A Vision of the Human Future in Space*, which was chosen as a notable book of 1995 by The *New York Times*.

26. **ANTHONY DE MELLO:** (1931 – 1987) was an Indian Jesuit priest and psychotherapist. A spiritual teacher, writer and public speaker, De Mello wrote several books on spirituality and hosted numerous spiritual retreats and conferences. He continues to be known for his unconventional approach to the priesthood and his storytelling which drew from the various mystical traditions of both East and West. De Mello was the oldest of five children born to Frank and Louisa née Castellino de Mello. He was born in Bombay, British India, on 4 September 1931. He was raised in a Catholic family and dreamed of one day joining the Jesuit order. As a teen, he entered the Society of Jesus in Bombay. He was ordained into the priesthood in March 1961. De Mello's first published book, *Sadhana - A way to God*, was released in 1978. It outlined a number of spiritual principles and "Christian exercises in eastern form" inspired by the teachings of Saint Ignatius. Other books published during his lifetime include *The Song of the Bird*, *One Minute Wisdom* and *Wellsprings*. The first two were collections of stories and the last a collection of exercises similar to *Sadhana*. In 1972,

he founded the Institute of Pastoral Counselling, later renamed
the Sadhana Institute of Pastoral Counseling, in Poona, India.

27. **NIKOS KAZANTZAKIS:** (1883 –1957) was a Greek
writer, celebrated for his novels, which include *Zorba the
Greek* (published 1946 as *Life and Times of Alexis Zorbas*),
Christ Recrucified (1948), *Captain Michalis* (1950, translated
'Freedom or Death), and *The Last Temptation of Christ* (1955).
He also wrote plays, travel books, memoirs and philosophical
essays such as *The Saviors of God: Spiritual Exercises.*
Universally recognised as a giant of modern Greek literature,
Kazantzakis was nominated for the Nobel Prize in Literature
in nine different years. His fame was further spread in the
English speaking world by cinematic adaptations of *Zorba the
Greek* (1964) and *The Last Temptation of Christ* (1988).

28. **ST. AUGUSTINE OF HIPPO:** (354 –430), also known as
Saint Austin, and the **Doctor of Grace**, was an early Christian
theologian and philosopher whose writings influenced the
development of Western Christianity and Western philosophy.
He was the bishop of Hippo Regius (modern-day Annaba,
Algeria). He is viewed as one of the most important Church
Fathers in Western Christianity for his writings in the Patristic
Era. Among his most important works are *The City of God* and
Confessions.

29. **ANANDA KENTIS COOMARASWAMI:** (1877-1947) was
a Ceylonese Tamil philosopher and metaphysician, as well as a
pioneering historian and philosopher of Indian art, particularly
art history and symbolism, a groundbreaking theorist and an
early interpreter of Indian culture to the West.

30. **BALINESE DANCE:** is a very ancient dance tradition, part
of religious and artistic expression among the Balinese people
of Bali Island in Indonesia. Balinese dance is dynamic, angular
and intensely expressive.

31. **JEAN-PAUL SATRE:** (1905 –1980) was a French
philosopher, playwright, novelist, political activist, biographer,
and embodied in his principal philosophical work *Being and*

Nothingness (*L'Être et le Néant*, 1943). Sartre's introduction to his philosophy is his work *Existentialism and Humanism* (*L'existentialisme est un humanisme*, 1946), originally presented as a lecture. He was awarded the 1964 Nobel Prize in Literature literary critic. He was one of the key figures in the philosophy of existentialism and phenomenology, and one of the leading figures in 20th-century French philosophy and Marxism. His play "*No Exit*" written and presented in 1944 became a hit with the most quoted sentence: "Hell is other people!" (L'enfer, c'est les autres!).

32. **GANDHI: Mohandas Karamchand Gandhi** (1869 –1948) was the preeminent leader of the Indian independence movement in British-ruled India. Employing nonviolent civil disobedience, Gandhi led India to independence and inspired movements for civil rights and freedom across the world. The honorific **Mahatma** applied to him first in 1914 in South Africa, is now used worldwide. He is also called **Bapu** (endearment for "father", "papa") in India. He is unofficially called the Father of the Nation. Eventually, in August 1947, Britain granted independence, but the British Indian Empire was partitioned into two dominions, a Hindu-majority India and Muslim Pakistan. As many displaced Hindus, Muslims, and Sikhs made their way to their new lands, religious violence broke out, especially in the Punjab and Bengal. Gandhi visited the affected areas, attempting to provide solace, he undertook several fasts unto death to promote religious harmony. Nathuram Godse, a Hindu nationalist, assassinated Gandhi on 30 January 1948 by firing three bullets into his chest at point-blank range. His birthday, 2 October, is commemorated as Gandhi Jayanti, a national holiday, and world-wide as the International Day of Nonviolence.

33. **JOHN DONNE:** an English poet famous with his poem **"No Man Is an Island"** from his 1624 work *Devotions upon Emergent Occasions*. The poem is as following:

No man is an island,

Entire of itself,
Every man is a piece of the continent,
A part of the main.
If a clod be washed away by the sea,
Europe is the less.
As well as if a promontory were.
As well as if a manor of thy friend's
Or of thine own were:
Any man's death diminishes me,
Because I am involved in mankind,
And therefore never send to know for whom the bell tolls;
It tolls for thee.

34.   **Albert Camus** (1913 –1960) was a French philosopher, author, and journalist. His views contributed to the rise of the philosophy known as absurdism. He wrote in his essay *The Rebel* that his whole life was devoted to opposing the philosophy of nihilism while still delving deeply into individual freedom. He won the Nobel Prize in Literature in 1957. Camus did not consider himself to be a follower of the existentialist ideology despite usually being classified as a follower of it, even in his lifetime. Camus was born in French Algeria, and graduated from the University of Algiers in 1936. In 1949, Camus founded the Group for International Liaisons to denounce two ideologies found in both the USSR and the USA.

35.   **THE BROTHERS KARAMAZOV:** is the final novel by the Russian author **Fyodor Dostoyevsky (1821-1881).** Dostoyevsky spent nearly two years writing *The Brothers Karamazov,* which was published as a serial in *The Russian Messenger* from January 1879 to November 1880. The author died less than four months after its publication. *The Brothers Karamazov* is a passionate philosophical novel set in 19th century Russia, that enters deeply into the ethical debates of God, free will, and morality. This is his largest work with 800 pages composed in 12 books. Since its publication, it has

been acclaimed as one of the supreme achievements in world literature. In this novel Zosima, a saintly monk, taught his novice, Alyosha, one of the three Karamazov brothers, that life is a paradise: "We do not understand that life is paradise, for it suffices only to wish to understand, and at once paradise will appear in front of us in its beauty."

36. **ST. JOHN OF THE CROSS:** (1542–1591) was a Spanish mystic, a Roman Catholic saint, a Carmelite friar and a priest who was born at Fontiveros, Old Castile. John of the Cross was a reformer in the Carmelite Order of his time and the movement he helped initiate, along with Saint Teresa of Ávila, eventually lead to the establishment of the Discalced Carmelites, though neither he nor Teresa were alive when the two orders separated. He is also known for his writings. Both his poetry and his studies on the growth of the soul are considered the summit of mystical Spanish literature and one of the peaks of all Spanish literature. Although his complete poems add up to fewer than 2500 verses, two of them — the *Spiritual Canticle* and the *Dark Night of the Soul* — are widely considered masterpieces of Spanish poetry, both for their formal stylistic point of view and their rich symbolism and imagery. His theological works often consist of commentaries on these poems. All the works were written between 1578 and his death in 1591, meaning there is great consistency in the views presented in them. He was canonized as a saint in 1726 by Pope Benedict XIII. He is one of the thirty-six Doctors of the Church.

37. **ST. BENEDICT:** (480-547) The Father of Western Monasticism and Patron of Europe. He was born in Norcia, Italy, and educated in Rome. He lived in the mountainous Subiaco for three years. Because there were many people requesting his guidance and wanting to be his disciples, he later organized them into twelve monasteries. In the abbey of Monte Casino which he found, he wrote his famous *Rule* which combines the Roman genius with the monastic wisdom. The monks devoted themselves to a life of moderate asceticism, prayer, study,

work and community life under one superior. Pope Paul the VI proclaimed him Patron of Europe because of his influence on the formation of Christendom.

38. **ST. THOMAS AQUINAS:** (1225-1274) was educated at the Benedictine abbey of Monte Casino during childhood and in the University of Naples when he was grown up and especially under St. Albert the Great. In 1244 he joined the Dominican Order. After having been ordained as priest in 1248, he taught in Paris, Rome, Naples and other cities, but his greatest contribution to the Church is his philosophical and theological writings. His monumental work of *Summa Theologica* has been used as text book even until today in seminaries. He is considered one of the greatest philosophers and theologians of all time and is called "Angelic Doctor".

39. Saint **Lawrence of Brindisi**, O.F.M. Cap. (1559 – 1619), born **Giulio Cesare Russo**, was a Roman Catholic priest and a theologian as well as a member of the Order of Friars Minor Capuchin. Giulio Cesare Russo was born in Brindisi, Kingdom of Naples, to a family of Venetian merchants. He was educated at Saint Mark's College in Venice, and joined the Capuchins in Verona as Brother Lawrence. He received further instruction from the University of Padua. An accomplished linguist, Lawrence spoke most European and Semitic languages fluently. He was appointed definitor general to Rome for the Capuchins in 1596; beginning in 1599, Lawrence established Capuchin monasteries in modern Germany and Austria. In 1601, he served as the imperial chaplain for the army of Rudolph II, Holy Roman Emperor, and successfully recruited Philippe Emmanuel, Duke of Mercœur to help fight against the Ottoman Turks. In 1602, he was elected vicar general of the Capuchin friars, at that time the highest office in the Order. He was elected again in 1605, but refused the office. He entered the service of the Holy See, becoming papal nuncio to Bavaria. After serving as nuncio to Spain, he retired to a monastery in 1618. He died on his birthday in Lisbon. He was beatified on 1 June 1783 and was canonized

as a saint on 8 December 1881. He was named a Doctor of the Church in 1959.

40.   **Saint John Cassian** (c. 360 – 435 AD), was a Christian monk and theologian celebrated in both the Western and Eastern Churches for his mystical writings. Cassian was born around 360, most likely in the region of Scythia Minor, a historical region shared today by Romania and Bulgaria. The son of wealthy parents, he received a good education. He was bilingual in Latin and Greek. As a young adult he and an older friend, Germanus, traveled to Palestine, where they entered a hermitage near Bethlehem. After remaining there for about three years, they journeyed to the desert of Scete in Egypt. There they visited a number of monastic foundations. In 415 Cassian accepted the invitation to found an Egyptian-style monastery in southern Gaul, near Marseilles. His foundation, the Abbey of St Victor, was a complex of monasteries for both men and women, one of the first such institutes in the West, and served as a model for later monastic development. Cassian's achievements and writings influenced St Benedict, who incorporated many of the principles into his monastic rule, and recommended to his own monks that they read the works of Cassian. Since Benedict's rule is still followed by Benedictine, Cistercian, and Trappist monks, John Cassian's thought still exercises influence over the spiritual lives of thousands of men and women today in the Latin Church. Cassian died in 435 at Marseille.

41.   **BASHO:** (1644-1694) the most famous poet in the Edo period in Japan. He was recognized the greatest master of haiku form (then called hokku). His notable work is *Oku no Hosomichi* . He made the living as a teacher, but then renounced the social and urban life and wandered throughout the country to gain inspiration for his writing.

APPENDIX 3

DISCUSSION GUIDE

Introduction

1. How do I understand Thomas Merton's concept of "the Paradise Man?"
2. Have I ever dreamt to live in a utopian world? Have I done anything in realizing the dream?
3. Have I ever reflected on my own existence, its meaning and its mission in the world?
4. How is my relationship with my Creator, my God?

Chapter One: Union with God

5. How do I experience God's immanence and transcendence?
6. The greatest gift of Baptism and other Sacraments is God's indwelling in my soul. Is that what God's immanence means?
7. How could I share this knowledge to my family members and friend about God's immanence in their personal lives? How do they experience God?
8. Through the Sacrament of the Eucharist, how do I experience God's immanence and God's transcendence?
9. What does it mean to be in union with God the Trinity in prayer?

Chapter Two: Union with the World

10. What is your favorite concept of The Paradise Man in ecology?
11. In what way do you practice stewardship of God's creation?
12. Have you ever been grateful to God as you experience God's creation?
13. Have you ever experienced the beauty of creation as a Paradise? Share your experience!

Chapter Three: Union with Humankind

14. Have you experienced a deep joy and love for yourself, your family and even for a stranger you met?
15. What are the practical things that we can do to alleviate human suffering?
16. Does your prayer life lead you into service?
17. How would you explain the biblical passage, "Faith without good works is dead?"
18. How do you feel and live the human world as the mystical body of Christ?
19. Have you ever met in your life anyone who lives and acts as a Paradise Man?

APPENDIX 4

NOTES

Introduction

1. Thomas Merton, *Conjectures of a Guilty Bystander*, P.118
2. The Thomas Merton Center at Bellarmine University: *merton. org /Thomas Merton's life and works.*
3. Thomas Merton, *Zen and the Birds of Appetite*, P.116
4. ibid, p. 116
5. Thomas Merton, *The Literary Essays of Thomas Merton*, p. 254
6. Thomas Merton, *New Seeds of Contemplation*, p.297

Chapter I

7. Thomas Merton, *The Silent Life*, p.2
8. ibid, p.3
9. Thomas Merton, *New Seeds of Contemplation*, pp. 282-283
10. ibid, p. 288
11. Teresa of Avila, *Interior Castle,* p.219
12. Thomas Merton, *He Is Risen*, p. 18
13. Thomas Merton, *New Seeds of Contemplation*, pp.286-287
14. ibid, p.286
15. ibid, p. 282
16. ibid, pp.287-288

17. Thomas Merton, *The New Man*, p.165
18. ibid, pp.167-168
19. ibid, p. 152
20. Teresa of Avila, *Interior Castle*, pp.106-107
21. Thomas Merton, *The Seven Storey Mountain*, p.170
22. Michael Cox, *Handbook of Christian Spirituality*, p.84
23. Thomas Merton, *New Seeds of Contemplation*, pp.283-284
24. Thomas Merton, *The Seven Storey Mountain*, pp.172-173
25. ibid, p.172
26. Thomas Merton, *Zen and the Birds of Appetite*, p. 79
27. Thomas Merton, *Love and Living*, p.180
28. ibid, p.180
29. Thomas Merton, *The Waters of Siloe*, p. XXI-XXII
30. Thomas Merton, *The New Man,* p.161
31. Teresa of Avila, *Interior Castle*, pp.33-35
32. Thomas Merton, *The Sign of Jonas*, p.246
33. ibid, p.272
34. Thomas Merton, *Thoughts in Solitude,* pp.99-100
35. Thomas Merton, *New Seeds of Contemplation*, p.266
36. Thomas Merton*, Life and Holiness*, p.30
37. ibid, pp. 30-31
38. Thomas Merton, *The New Man*, pp.174-175
39. Thomas Merton, *Thoughts in Solitude*, pp.123-124
40. Thomas Merton, *Zen and the Birds of Appetite*, p.57
41. Abishiktananda (Henry Le Saux), *Prayer,* p.6
42. ibid, pp.18-19
43. Thomas Merton, *Thoughts in Solitude*, pp.122-123
44. Teresa of Avila, *Interior Castle*, p.199
45. Thomas Merton, *The Seven Storey Mountain*, p.87
46. Thomas Merton, *The Waters of Siloe*, p.4

Chapter II

47. Thomas Merton, *New Seeds of Contemplation*, p.25
48. Thomas Merton, *Love and Living*, p.51

49. ibid, p.53

50. Thomas Merton, *The Sign of Jonas*, p.92

51. Thomas Merton, *Day of a Stranger*, p.49

52. Fyodor Dostoyevsky, *The Brothers Karamazov*, Vol. I, pp. 375, 376

53. Thomas Merton, *Day of a Stranger*, p.33

54. Thomas Merton, *Raids on the Unspeakable*, pp.93-94

55. Carl Sagan, *A Pale Blue Dot*, Random House, New York, 1994

56. Anthony de Mello, *The Song of the Birds*, p.17

57. Thomas Merton, *Collected Poems*: "The Fall", p.355

58. Nikos Kazantzakis, *Report to Greco*, P.430

59. Thomas Merton, *New Seeds of Contemplation*, pp. 29-30

60. ibid, p.30

61. Thomas Merton, *Thoughts in Solitude*, p.94

62. Thomas Merton, *Bread in the Wilderness*, p.50

63. Thomas Merton, *Dancing in the Water of Life*, p.187

64. Thomas Merton, *The New Man*, pp.57

65. Fyodor Dostoyevsky, *The Brothers Karamazov*, Vol. I, p. 346

66. Thomas Merton, *The New Man*, pp.80-81

67. Thomas Merton, *No Man is an Island*, p.100

68. Thomas Merton, *The Literary Essays of T.M.*, p.364

69. ibid, p.365

70. ibid, p.369

71. ibid, p.370

72. Fyodor Dostoyevsky, *The Brothers Karamazov*, Vol. I, p.346

Chapter III

73. Thomas Merton, *The Seven Storey Mountain*, pp.413-414

74. William H. Shannon, "Thomas Merton and the Discovery of the Real Self ", *Cistercian Studies Series*, No. 42, p.200

75. Thomas Merton, *Gandhi and Non-Violence*, p.6

76. Thomas Merton, *No Man is an Island*, Prologue, pp. XXII-XXIII

77. Thomas Merton, *The Waters of Siloe*, Prologue, p. XVIII

78.	Thomas Merton, "A Letter on 'Disinterested Love'", *Seeds of Destruction*, p.261

79.	Thomas Merton, *The Seven Storey Mountain*, p.57

80.	Thomas Merton, *The New Man*, p.91

81.	Thomas Merton, *The Waters of Siloe*, pp.22-25

82.	Thomas Merton, *Zen and the Birds of Appetite*, p.62

83.	Albert Camus, *Notebooks*, New York, Alfred A. Knoff,1935-1942, p.54; Cf. *The Literary Essays of Thomas Merton*

p.241

84.	Thomas Merton, *The Nonviolent Alternative*, pp.222-223

85.	Thomas Merton, *He is Risen*, p.8

86.	ibid, p.9

87.	Thomas Merton, *New Seeds of Contemplation*, p.263

88.	Thomas Merton, *Zen and the Birds of Appetite*, p.116

89.	Thomas Merton, *Thoughts in Solitude*, p.43

90.	ibid, p.44

91.	ibid, p.122

92.	Thomas Merton, *Zen and the Birds of Appetite*, p.51

93.	ibid, p. 115

94.	Thomas Merton, *The Seven Storey Mountain*, pp. 422-423

95.	Thomas Merton, *New Seeds of Contemplation*, p.71

96.	Thomas Merton, *Zen and the Birds of Appetite*, p.114

97.	Thomas Merton, *The New Man*, p.155

98.	Thomas Merton, *The Seven Storey Mountain*, p.348

99.	ibid, pp. 313-314

100.	Thomas Merton, *New Seeds of Contemplation*, pp.192-193

101.	Thomas Merton, *The Waters of Siloe*, p.XXXVII

102.	Thomas Merton, *The Seven Storey Mountain*, p.419

103.	Thomas Merton, *New Seeds of Contemplation*, p.193

104.	Thomas Merton, *Gandhi on Non-Violence*, p.5

105.	ibid, p.8

106.	ibid, p.10

107.	ibid, p.10

108.	ibid, p.6

109. ibid, p.8
110. Thomas Merton, *New Seeds of Contemplation*, p.250
111. Thomas Merton, *The Seven Storey Mountain*, p.383
112. Thomas Merton, *Mystics and Zen Masters*, p.75
113. Thomas Merton, *The Silent Life*, p.6
114. Thomas Merton, *New Seeds of Contemplation*, p.150
115. Thomas Merton, *Life and Holiness*, p.54
116. Thomas Merton, *Bread in the Wilderness*, p.85
117. Thomas Merton, *The Silent Life*, pp.168-169
118. Thomas Merton, *The New Man*, p.148
119. ibid, p.148
120. ibid, pp. 136-137
121. http:// *Kolbecenter.org/*
122. ibid

Conclusion

123. Thomas Merton, *Conjectures by a Guilty Bystander*, p.118
124. William Benton Publisher. *Encyclopedia Britannica*, Volume 22, p.913
125. Thomas Merton, *The Silent Life*, p.13
126. Thomas Merton, *Selected Essays*, p.59
127. Ibid, p.59
128. Ibid, p.63
129. Thomas Merton, *New Seeds of Contemplation*. pp. 296-297

APPENDIX 5

BIBLIOGRAPHY

Benton, William, Publisher. *Encyclopedia Britannica*, Volume 22. Chicago: London: Toronto. 1960 edition

Camus, Albert. *Notebooks*. New York: Alfred A. Knoff, 1935

Cox, Michael. *A Handbook of Christian Spirituality*. San Francisco: Harper & Row, 1983

De Mello, Anthony. *The Song of the Bird*. Anand, India: Gujarat Sahitya Prakash Publisher, 1982

Dostoyevski, Fyodor. *The Brothers Karamazov*. from D. Magarshak's translation. Penguin edition, 1958). Quoted by Rudolf Neuhauser, University of Klagenfurt, in article "The Brothers Karamazov, A Contemporary Reading of Book VI, "A Russian Monk"; by © International Dostoevsky Society University of Toronto: The Department of Slavic Languages and Literatures.

Kazantzakis, Nikos. *Report to Greco*. New York: Bantam Books,1966

Le Saux, Henri (Abishiktananda). *Prayer*. Philadelphia: Westminster Press,1973

Merton, Thomas. *The Asian Journal of Thomas Merton*. New York: New Directions Publisher, 1975

Merton, Thomas. *Bread in the Wilderness*. Collegeville, Minnesota:The Liturgical Press, 1971

Merton, Thomas. *Dancing in the Water of Life*. Edited by Robert Daggy. San Francisco Harper, 1997

Merton, Thomas. *Day of a Stranger*. Salt Lake City: Gibbs M. Smith Inc., 1981

Merton, Thomas. *Gandhi and Non Violence*. New York: New Directions Publishing Co., 1965

Merton, Thomas. *He is Risen*. Allen, Texas: Argus Communication, 1975

Merton, Thomas. *Mystics and Zen Masters*. New York: Dell Publishing Co. Inc., 1980

Merton, Thomas. *Life and Holiness*. New York: Image Publisher, 1964

Merton, Thomas. *The Literary Essays of Thomas Merton*. Edited by Patrick Hart, New York: New Directions Publishing Co. 1985

Merton, Thomas. *Love and Living*. Edited by Naomi Burton Stone and Br. Patrick Hart, New York: Farrar, Straus, and Giroux, 1979

Merton, Thomas. *The New Man*. New York: Farrar, Straus and Giroux, 1981

Merton, Thomas. *New Seeds of Contemplation*. New York: New Direction Publishing Co., 1972

Merton, Thomas. *The Nonviolent Alternative*. New York: Farrar, Straus, and Giroux, 1980

Merton, Thomas. *No Man is an Island*. New York and London: Harcourt, Brace, Jovanovich Publishers, 1978

Merton, Thomas. *Raids of the Unspeakable*. New York: New Directions Publishing Co. 1964

Merton, Thomas. *Seeds of Destruction*. New York: Farrar, Straus, and Giroux, 1980

Merton, Thomas. *Thomas Merton: Selected Essays*. Edited by Patrick F. O'Connell. New York, Maryknoll: Orbis Books, 2013

Merton, Thomas. *The Seven Storey Mountain*. New York: Harcourt, Brace, Jovanovich, Publisher 1978

Merton, Thomas. *The Sign of Jonas*. New York: Harcourt, Brace, Jovanovich, Publishers, 1979

Merton, Thomas. *The Silent Life.* New York: Harcourt, Brace Jovanovich, Publishers, 1981

Merton, Thomas. *Thoughts in Solitude.* New York: Farrar, Straus, and Giroux, 1981

Merton, Thomas. *The Waters of Siloe.* New York: Harcourt Brace, Jovanovich, Publishers 1979

Merton, Thomas. *Zen and the Birds of Appetite.* New York: New Directions Publishing Co., 1986

Sagan, Carl. A Pale Blue Dot. New York: Random House, 1994

Sartre, Jean-Paul. *No Exit*, one act play. Paris, 1994

St. Teresa of Avila, *Interior Castle.* Garden City, New York: Image, Doubleday, 1961

PERIODICALS

Cistercian Studies Series, Kalamazoo, Michigan: Cistercian Publications, 1981. No. 42, Articles: "Thomas Merton's Glimpse of the Kingdom" by James Douglas and "Thomas Merton and the Recovery of the Real Self" by William Shannon

WEBSITES

http://www.space.com
http://www.dailygalaxy.com
http://www.universetoday.com
http://Kolbecenter.org/Christ-the-exemplar-cause-of-creation-eliminates-the-possibility-of-evolution
http://www.merton.org/Thomas Merton's life and works